ABOVE GROUND LEVEL

The Story of Stuart Bell

A Biography by Ralph Turner

Ralph Turner

malcolm down

PUBLISHING

First published 2022 by Malcolm Down Publishing Ltd

www.malcolmdown.co.uk

25 24 23 22   7 6 5 4 3 2 1

British Library Cataloguing in Publication Data
A catalogue record for this book is available from the British Library.

ISBN 978-1-915046-45-1

Cover design by Esther Kotecha

Art direction by Sarah Grace

COMMENDATIONS

Stuart and Irene Bell have made a huge contribution to the life and health of the British church and beyond. Here are stories of breakthrough and victory that need to be told. But true faith shines when faithfulness is demanded for the darker days. Through tearful, fearful seasons, they have trusted Jesus. Their story will challenge, inspire and gently nudge us into hope. A must read.

Jeff Lucas
Author, Speaker, Broadcaster

All those who know Stuart Bell will be enthralled with the stories in this book. It is about a godly, self-effacing leader. I am honoured to have been a small part of Stuart's life. This book takes me back on a nostalgic journey during which some of the best people on earth became my friends.

RT Kendall
Minister of Westminster Chapel, 1977–2002

I'm so pleased that this biography has been written. Stuart's life is a story that needs telling and I am thankful to Ralph Turner for writing so well.

I have known Stuart for almost 40 years and worked very closely with him for much of that time. Stuart has always been passionate to follow the work of the Holy Spirit, pursue unity and build strong relationships. His life, along with his wife Irene, has impacted multiple thousands over the years and I too, along with my family, fall into that category.

As you read this story, I am certain that you will be impacted and that something of Stuart's vision, heart and anointing will minister to you. Stuart is a true apostolic leader who has served his generation well in the will of God. I fully recommend this biography to you.

Paul Benger
Lead Pastor of Ikon Church and Leader of the Ground Level Network of Churches

Stuart and Irene's story is one of faith and faithfulness. And, because no one is more faithful than our God, it is one of incredible fruitfulness as well. At a time when the Church needs leaders who can lead with great vision, godly wisdom and gentle authority, these are lives that should inspire and instruct us all.

Paul Harcourt
National Leader, New Wine England

Revivals have come and gone through history . . . but someone must tell the story. It is the story of the Holy Spirit stirring the heart of a man or woman . . . and then those persons choosing to believe God.

We can argue for hours what causes revival, but revivals burn as the baton is passed, the stories of old are told . . . 'Lord, I have heard of your fame; I stand in awe of your deeds, repeat them in our day . . .'

My friend Ralph is the storyteller of revivals, and Stuart and Irene those who have given their lives because they believe God. The story continues whenever the next stirred heart takes the baton.

Steve Barber
Senior Pastor, Chroma Church

Stuart Bell is a man who has pioneered a network of leaders and churches in the UK; that has transitioned through the early house church movement, followed by the early Charismatic days, then the large summer camps and celebrations, until today. His story is one of resolute courage, sensitivity to the Holy Spirit, while learning how to endure pain and betrayal along the way. This is a book that will inspire you to lead, challenge you to take risks and endure hardships, while also making you smile. Both Stuart and Irene have been instrumental in many lives, and we are richer for their wisdom.

Rachel Hickson
Founder of Heartcry for Change, Oxford, UK

I have always been impressed by Stuart's style of leadership. This book now fills in the details. It has me wishing I could have drawn on Stuart's experience when facing my leadership challenges and been there for him as he faced his. I strongly believe that many in leadership will be deeply encouraged by Stuart's and Irene's story and be grateful to God that none of us has to travel alone. This is a story in which friendships, family life and ministry relationships constantly shine through. May we each build our own strong relationship inspired by Stuart and Irene's testimony.

Hugh Osgood
Past-President, Churches Together in England

This is a timely biography of a man who puts God first. From his early days with the band through to his oversight of a whole church movement, Stuart had sought to listen to the Spirit and obey the Word. I recommend this highly readable biography.

Debra Green OBE
Executive Director, Redeeming Our Communities

Surely one of the best descriptions ever given of a person was when Jesus said of Nathaniel, 'Behold, an Israelite indeed, in whom there is no deceit' (John 1:47). He stood out amongst his compatriots as the real deal with no sense of falsehood. I've often felt this is also an accurate description of Stuart Bell.

There has been a lot of talk in recent times about authenticity and how important it is in today's world which has more than its fair share of phoneys, and this sadly includes within the Church. Thank God for leaders like Stuart who have demonstrated something different over the long haul. A true Lincolnite in whom there's nothing false.

Enjoy this insightful and honest read as you learn of the real Stuart from boyhood to a wise master builder who it was clear was set apart to play a significant part in God's purpose in our times. The Church is richer, and many lives are the better because of Stuart Bell.

Steve Campbell
Senior Pastor, The C3 Church UK and National Director, GLNUKI

Stuart has been an amazingly faithful friend and support for such a long time and has also stood faithfully as an advisor to KingsGate over many decades. As well as building a great church in Lincoln, establishing a strong network of churches, and leading the Grapevine/One Event celebrations, Stuart has an extraordinary capacity to generously invest in leaders and churches in the wider body of Christ. I'm thrilled that this book is going to tell his life story.

Dave Smith
Senior Pastor, KingsGate Church

This story speaks of a man of humility and service, filled with a radical love for Jesus and His Church. It was a highlight of my year to get to read it. It is clear that God's intention in calling Stuart was to leave a lasting legacy in the lives of others, many of whom he would never meet. I am one such person.

I grew up in a 1980s house church, inspired by those like Stuart who pioneered the movement. I attended Hull University and led a Christian Union profoundly affected by his visit just a few years earlier. And in 2005 I attended Grapevine with my future wife Abi, where we both independently received a call from God to serve the church, subsequently planting and leading churches in the city of Hull.

Stuart's heart for the Humber to the Wash is still very much on God's heart and we long for the same move of God's Spirit in revival. Stuart and Irene, thank you for winning so many battles on our behalf, and thank you for discipling sons and daughters in Christ that you never even met.

John Flavell
Church Leader, River City Church, Hull

The Church in the West has traversed five decades in which its culture has shifted from sleepiness to awakening, to proliferation, to refreshing, and finally, and maybe unfortunately, to celebrity. It is a novel thing, then, to consider the life of a man and a ministry that has weathered those shifts with a consistency of humility and godly character such that a statesman of sorts has arisen. Stuart Bell is that man. So then this, his story, is a life well worth considering and emulating in an age that needs to train its eyes upon those who actually finish well.

Jack Groblewski
Pastor Emeritus, NC4 Church

7

Thank You

As always, with a task like this there are many to thank.

First of all, my thanks to Stuart and Irene Bell for the hours of interviews both in Lincoln and via video calls. I'm grateful for the welcome and friendship I received.

My thanks, too, to all those that I interviewed in person or on video: Andrew Bell, Becki Ross, Dave Bell, Pete Atkins, Chris and Lesley Bowater, Caroline Cameron, Jack and Trish Groblewski, John Hindmarsh, Dave Kitchen, Jeff Lucas and Duane White. Special thanks to Dave Kitchen for the excellent archive material relating to The Advocates. Thank you to Lois Delong, Stuart's PA, for the management of Stuart's interviews.

Thank you as always to my wife Roh, who accompanied me on the trips to Lincoln and to the One Event. And thanks, too, to my proofreaders Nathan Turner and Alison Leigh. I'm grateful as well for the additional proofreading duties taken on by Andrew Bell. Editing from Louise Stenhouse is, as always, first class.

A shout out and thanks for the encouragement to Chroma Church, Leicester.

And thank you again Malcolm Down and Sarah Grace for your ongoing belief in my writing.

Ralph Turner

CONTENTS

Introduction   13

Chapter One – The Bible Before he Could Read   15

Chapter Two – The Advocates   30

Chapter Three – The Journey   46

Chapter Four – Church by Accident   59

Chapter Five – The Vision and The Call   73

Chapter Six – The Freedom and The Fire   87

Chapter Seven – The Spirit and The Servant   114

Chapter Eight – Living in the Good   131

Chapter Nine – The Turn of a Page   148

Chapter Ten – The Testing and the Trials   158

Chapter Eleven – Heritage   170

Chapter Twelve – The End of the Beginning   181

End-Piece By Stuart Bell   190

Introduction

There's a determination and discipline to the start of Stuart's day. The alarm wakes him at 7.00am. It's on with the running shoes and out of the door. Down the country lane, around the marina, across the fields and into the woods, before heading home.

Each day. Every day. The same start. The same rhythm.

His pace is short, reflecting his five-foot-seven-inch frame. His steps are steady, regular, determined.

Each step reflects a prayer. Starting with Irene, his wife of just over fifty years, on through his three children, Andrew, Rebekah and Dave, together with their own families. Then the church leaders at Alive Church, Lincoln, the church he and Irene have had the privilege of leading for over thirty years. Then the Ground Level leaders – his friends and colleagues in the movement that is part of his Christian journey, each representing their own churches and ministries in this move of God.

Each one. Each step. Each prayer. Pushing through.

Road. Water. Meadow. Trees.

The terrain itself a reflection of the different seasons to Stuart and Irene's lives of service to God. Times of wide-open spaces. Times of being hemmed in between the trees with little to guide as to the path to take.

And home again. A shower, a coffee, and a book. The well-worn pages of Stuart's study Bible are open on the patio table. This morning it's warm enough to be out on the decking, overlooking the lake. A good place to live. A tranquil setting, comforting, quietening, easing into the day.

And today is a little different. His good friend Gerald Coates' phone call a few weeks earlier has been carefully considered, prayed through, stepped through on that early morning run.

Gerald had a dream. In it he saw Stuart and his life mapped out in front of him. And as he woke, there was a sense that Stuart needed to tell his story, to put it into print. It was to be one of the last contacts from Gerald, who stepped over the finish line himself during the completion of this book.

Gerald's suggestion is counter-intuitive to Stuart. Never one to boast, he doesn't consider his story to be particularly newsworthy. But then, on reflection, there is so much that could be said. The Christian band, the outreaches, the church, the movement of churches that has been birthed from the careful, steady, running of a man seeking God and His purposes.

So, yes, there is a story to be told. And today it begins. The visit of a Christian author and his wife to discuss a biography. The start of a journey to tell of a journey. The start of a narrative of praise to a God who has answered prayer, who has led, supported, comforted and empowered.

One step at a time.

Chapter One
The Bible Before He Could Read

'Come on, Stuart, we don't want to be late. If you're only ten minutes early, you're already late!'

Young Stuart was coming down the stairs, struggling to put on his smart Macintosh over his best clothes.

Harmonium Church

This was such a treat for Stuart. At six years of age, to be given a late-night pass to travel with his dad to the evening church meetings. And better still, to be allowed to sit on the crossbar of Dad's bike to get there.

Dad was a lay preacher for the Methodist Church. Based at Carholme Road Methodist Church, in the same area of Lincoln the family lived in, he served by travelling to various congregations to preach and teach on Sunday evenings, occasionally a Wednesday or Thursday night Bible study too. The meetings themselves were rather small. Often just a handful of older folk, with an old lady playing a harmonium. Singing Wesleyan hymns that started slowly and then sped up as the harmonium player got carried away with the words. Gathering in a circle for the Bible study that Dad would lead.

Quaint. Outdated. But Stuart loved it. From a young age he'd had a sense of God's presence and a love for God's Word. Dad spoke well, but the best evenings would be when he would play reel-to-reel tapes of others teaching. The Word of God was finding a place in a young boy's heart from an early age.

Stuart's earliest memory is of being in a big-wheeled pram, with Mum pushing him up Lower Long Leys Hill. There are a lot of hills in Lincoln. Strong leg muscles are par for the course – or for the hills, as it were. Mum and Dad were keen that Stuart exercised his mind as well as his legs and reading the Bible was very much part of family life. Learning to read and learning to walk came together in the Bell household.

First Bible

The first Bible Stuart received was from his parents. He remembers it to this day. A soft-back leather cover with each book of the Bible having an indentation in order to find things quickly. The funny thing was, he was so young he couldn't easily read it! But just to have such a gift as a six-year-old was wonderful to him. Even though he couldn't yet read it – especially the King James English of the version he was given – the Bible made a significant impact on him. A book to be treasured. And later on, one to be diligently studied.

Alongside those early Bibles were the reel-to-reel tapes of course. One set that particularly hit home to Stuart while he was still only seven or eight years old was a set of teaching tapes from Francis Dixon. Pastor at Lansdowne Baptist Church in Bournemouth, Francis Dixon sent out tapes around the country, along with printed Bible study notes, and Stuart remembers making his own notes alongside the printed ones. Francis Dixon would go through books of the Bible verse by verse, and each talk would usually carry three main points. For those that know Stuart today, the three-point sermon approach may well bring his latest sermon to mind!

Methodist socials were regular events for the Bell family, alongside special occasions such as the Christmas celebration – including one year when the minister, in lighting a candle, set the whole Christmas tree on fire!

Sunday school was a requirement for the Bell children, and for older brother Graham, along with Stuart, it was preceded by Boys' Brigade at 9.00am. Stuart and close friend John Hindmarsh attended Junior Christian Endeavour. Sunday school summer trips were woven into the fabric of growing up, with Sutton-on-Sea and Mablethorpe being the preferred destinations. Always a highlight of the year.

As Stuart grew, Sunday school morphed into Youth Club. Monday nights at the local church, Friday nights at Central Methodist Hall in the heart of Lincoln.

It was Saint Francis Xavier who made the now famous comment, 'Give me the children until they are seven and anyone may have them afterward.' His meaning, of course, was that they could be shaped and nurtured in the things of God in such a way in their early years that they would never lose their early faith.

Discipline

The same is true for Stuart. It was a slightly rigid, disciplined upbringing but one filled with prayer and praise, supported by godly parents and grandparents. An upbringing that honoured God and one that loved His Word. For young Stuart, younger sister Elizabeth and brother Graham (three years his senior), it did mean that Sundays could seem a bit starchy and formal. No games or football allowed. Best clothes all day. Sunday church meetings aside, Stuart remembers looking forward to Mondays at school when football *was* allowed!

Strict, but not over-strict. Cousin Dave remembers the children being sent into the front room after lunch on Christmas Day at the Bell household. They were told to behave themselves and, for a while, managed to do so, playing a board game. But disagreements led to cushion fights and on more than one occasion during those early Christmases as kids, ornaments were broken – and later retribution exacted!

Sundays may have been stricter, but Saturdays were not. The family owned an allotment, set next to another owned by Stuart's aunt and uncle. As children, they would be there most Saturdays, working the two allotments, often taking it in turn to push a small handheld plough and later pulling the produce home in a small contraption connected to their bikes. The kids thought it was fun. The adults were pleased that they did!

Football

Football was a big thing for the young and growing Stuart. He was good. Often captaining his school year teams at St Faith's Infant School and, later, playing at The City School, the grammar school he attended. He even got a trial at Lincoln City Boys.

There was a problem though. A five-foot-seven-inch problem. Stuart was a small and skinny youth. It meant he was easily pushed off the ball and simply wasn't tall enough to reach the headers in the penalty area.

It didn't bother him that much. He'd still be out in the street, playing on into the evening and through to the eventual call to go to bed. John Hindmarsh was his friend and football companion most of the time. They were in the same class at St Faith's and remained together in secondary school too. John was also an attender at the Carholme Road Methodist Church, and later at West Parade Methodist when the Carholme building closed. He and Stuart would usually be found on the back pews during the Sunday morning meetings. Sometimes they'd be listening. Sometimes they'd be talking about football. And as they grew, sometimes they'd be acting up and showing off to the girls.

The Beatles

If it wasn't football, it was music, specifically The Beatles. Stuart was captivated, not just by the melodies but by the words. There was a depth to The Beatles' lyrics, especially as the 1960s rolled into its latter half. Songs about the short time we have on this earth. Even today you may hear Stuart allude to these lyrics as he's preaching.

As the children grew and became tired of working on the allotment on Saturdays, music became more important and visits to the local record shop took pride of place.

Spouges Record Store, Lincoln, boasted the latest technology. Individual booths where you could share headphones and listen to the top ten of the day. Stuart and John spent many an hour there. John remembers listening to the new Tremeloes single, along with hits from Gerry and the Pacemakers, The Who and the Rolling Stones. But as always, it was The Beatles' latest they wanted to listen to first.

Sharing their peanuts purchased at Woolworths, the two would remain in the store for as long as they could, before moving next door to the roller-skating rink to finish their day together.

Not all these childhood activities were quite so innocent though. John recalls he and Stuart purchasing stink bombs from the local joke shop and setting them off in Woolworths before making a quick exit.

It wasn't all The Beatles in the Bell household either. Older brother Graham was a classical music buff from an early age, going on to play the organ and the French horn. Elizabeth, Stuart's younger sister by seven years, was growing up with the next generation of pop music.

Whether it was Methodist hymns, pop or classical, the music pervading the family home had its effect. Starting in his early years, pretending to be Ringo, playing drums on a tin can, Stuart progressed onto the guitar and keyboards. Having managed the guitar fairly easily, keyboards was more of a challenge. There was a piano in the lounge and practice became a regular event.

All the hard work was finding an outlet as well.

'Hey, Stu! Stuart!'

John came running up as Stuart was walking home from school.

'I've said I'd help at Youth Group on Sunday. Do you fancy helping me? I thought maybe we'd teach them a couple of the *Youth Praise* songs we were practising. And maybe we could sing them that song we were working on from The Overcomers' album?'

And so it began. The first tentative steps into performance.

Holidays

Serious practice would follow, but in those early days it was just fun to be together with friends. Before Stuart and John ever picked up a guitar, their interest in music was obvious. They were always the first to sign up to attend the various Methodist music festivals and observe the music competitions that were part of the summer calendar throughout Lincolnshire. As they grew and guitars were purchased, Stuart and John started to enter the music competitions themselves. Good friends, but also rivals, often they would be placed first and second in the competitions, each belting out the songs set by the adjudicators.

John lived across the road and would be around the house a lot of the time, especially when Stuart's mum had made a batch of her homemade orange ice lollies. There wasn't a lot of room to play or to practise. An end-of-terrace three-bedroom house, built before the Second World War, things were pretty basic. The toilet was in the back yard, the kitchen tiny. The house did not boast central heating until a lot later in Stuart's childhood, and hot water for baths had to be heated as and when required. Carpet was reserved for the front room, with most of the house clad in linoleum; cold to the feet and a little unwelcoming.

There was nothing unwelcoming about the family though. John was always greeted with delight by stay-at-home mum. Dad, when not serving in the Methodist Church, was away at work during the week; long hours with heavy machinery as an engineer. Later on in life he changed career completely and became part-owner of a Christian bookshop in Lincoln.

Holidays as a family were almost always in the same place. A Christian guest house in Bridlington, on the coast and a couple of hours north of Lincoln was the home-away-from-home for the last week of August throughout Stuart, Graham and Elizabeth's childhood. Mum and Dad loved it. It was a bit of a step up from local Skegness and had the advantage of Christian meetings during the week.

It was a Christian meeting of a different kind that got Stuart's attention. For much of the summer holidays, students from Cliff College, a Christian institution based in Derbyshire, were on the beach at Bridlington. Open-air evangelism included drama and games and was definitely the place Stuart and Graham wanted to go as soon as the family arrived at the beach. On Sundays there was an open-air service attended by the family – Dad in those days was a little conflicted as to what was allowed on the 'Sabbath' so would sit in his deckchair dressed in suit and tie.

Billy Graham Meetings

Surrounded by Christian family and with the extra input from others such as the Cliff College students meant that Stuart was very aware of God in his life. But even so, there was a particular night. At fourteen years old, Stuart found himself in the Central Methodist Hall in Lincoln.

The words that night, spoken by John Wesley White, a Billy Graham Association evangelist, were not new. But what was new was a compelling sense that they were aimed directly at Stuart.

The meeting was well attended. It would have been easy to hide, easy to ignore what was being said. After all, hadn't he always been a Christian? For as long as he could remember, he'd believed in Jesus.

It was a straightforward presentation of the gospel, but to fourteen-year-old Stuart, everything came together on that day. There it was. The call on his life. A call to repentance and a call to serve. A call to make his life count. He *had* to respond.

Leaning forward in the pew, feeling tearful, Stuart listened to every word. He needed to be sure. He needed to know that he was

God's son. And he needed to say 'yes' to the call on his life. Always suspected but never responded to, Stuart knew at that moment that he would be serving God in some kind of full-time capacity in the future.

When the invitation to go forward came, Stuart was quickly out of his seat.

It was a confirming moment. One that he knew meant giving everything to God. And one that God saw; a moment where He met Stuart in a gentle and affirming way. A son called to serve. A son giving all to his Father. A life to be lived in service to the One who sent His Son to die for him. A life forgiven and free.

He may only be five feet and seven inches, and shorter still as a fourteen-year-old, but when Stuart left Central Methodist Hall that night, he felt six-foot tall.

Lincoln

When was it that Stuart knew he was to remain in Lincoln, that this was the place God had called him to? The thing is, there really wasn't a moment. There was no sudden revelation, no 'God spoke to me' instant. It was simply a growing revelation that the city of Lincoln was the city God had placed on Stuart's heart. 'Stuartoflincoln' is the Twitter handle for Stuart and totally appropriate.

Part of that calling to Lincoln came from Stuart's upbringing. The family were not ambitious in their travels – in fact Mum and Dad had only travelled abroad once in their lives; a trip to Israel. They had a close-knit community around them and a church that they knew and loved. And for Stuart, it wasn't so much 'God, where do you want me?' but 'God, how can I serve you where I am?' Looking back now, Stuart sees that he always had a love for the city, though in his younger years he would not have seen it as clearly as that.

When it came to university, there was no great desire to leave home. Music was taking off. The church was growing. So rather than further education, Stuart joined the Health Department of Lindsey County Council – the same place cousin Dave worked. With seven O Levels and two good A Levels under his belt, he went on to study for a Higher National Certificate in Public Administration.

On his first day in the office he was welcomed by Arthur Mann, a fellow Christian and someone who was about to turn Stuart's life upside down.

'This Man is a Christian, Listen to Him!'

Arthur Mann was quite a character.

First there was a tour of the offices. Through the administration department to the typing pool. The clatter of the typewriters made it hard to hear Arthur. The smoke from the numerous cigarettes made it difficult to breathe! Eventually they ended up in the health department office Stuart was to work in as a Section Head.

Arthur, being aware of Stuart's faith, was just about to put his witness at work in absolutely no doubt.

As Arthur and Stuart arrived in the health department that morning, Arthur did something that may seem outlandish. Waiting for a lull in conversation, Arthur shouted out to the fifteen or so people in the office.

'Hey, everyone, this is Stuart. He's starting today in this department. This man is a Christian, listen to him!'

And with that, he left.

Instant embarrassment. What to do, what to say.

Stuart smiled, waved a 'hello' and sat down at his new desk.

But something was broken in that moment. Any shyness, any reticence to speak about Jesus was gone. Stuart would be known as part of the 'God Squad' and was happy for it to be so. His faith being announced meant that it would be so much easier to talk about Jesus to his colleagues.

Baptism in the Spirit

Arthur Mann's influence doesn't end there, either. He was part of a Pentecostal congregation in the city and also led a small fellowship of his own. Injured in the Korean War with significant facial injuries, God had miraculously healed Arthur and, as a result, he was fearless in his faith.

He was also baptised in the Holy Spirit.

Stuart was intrigued by the full-on nature of Arthur's faith. What was it that accounted for that?

At the time, coming from a Methodist background, baptism in the Holy Spirit was not something on Stuart's radar. But as he chatted with Arthur, he became more and more aware of the need for the Holy Spirit in his life.

By now, cousin and long-time friend Dave Kitchen was also working for the council. Dave was not so open and debated the baptism in the Holy Spirit with Arthur over a number of lunch breaks, arguing that this baptism was no longer for today.

Stuart and Dave had experienced speaking in tongues at one or two churches where they had been invited to sing. Dave remembers Stuart being asked to pray in one of the meetings and, as he began, the whole congregation began to pray with him, often drowning his voice as they cried out and spoke in tongues. Neither had known what to make of it at the time.

Arthur suggested that the best way forward would be to spend some time together one evening, where he could more fully explain the baptism and tell of his own story.

Dave wasn't too keen and chose not to go at first, but was then baptised in the Holy Spirit in a powerful way while out on business with Arthur Mann.

The meeting was at their friend Keith's house. Stuart and John were present, curious to know what this baptism in the Spirit was all about.

It's a bit of a generalisation, but for many years the baptism in the Holy Spirit was seen to be something that related only to the Pentecostal churches – both the Elim and Assemblies of God denominations found their roots back in the Azusa Street revivals in Los Angeles in the early 1900s.

But as the 1970s came into view, God was about a new thing in the British Isles. Many from other denominations were finding that the infilling of the Holy Spirit was real and life changing. In the Anglican Church, the Fountain Trust group, led by Michael Harper, was openly teaching on it. Arthur Wallis, in the early days of forming the house church movement, had found the baptism in the Holy Spirit to be both true and transforming. Books such as Denis Bennett's *Nine O'Clock in the Morning* were doing the rounds, challenging the concept that the Holy Spirit baptism was solely for the early church.

And it was into this background of a growing acceptance of the baptism that Arthur Mann found a receptive audience.

That evening he spoke of his own story and took his listeners through the Pentecost story too. Arthur asked his friends to pray out loud. Again, this was new to Stuart, not something that was regularly done outside of formal meetings in the Methodist Church. Arthur encouraged each of them to pray and make sure that they were clean vessels ready to be filled. This included repentance from any known sin.

Stuart prayed his best general prayer.

'Stuart, that's not good enough,' said Arthur. 'Be specific. Ask God for forgiveness for sins you know you have committed.'

Well, this was getting embarrassing! Nevertheless, Stuart stepped out and sought specific forgiveness for the things he remembered doing.

It was this openness that helped with what was to follow.

Having led everyone in very clear prayers of repentance, Arthur went on to explain.

'There's nothing stopping you from receiving the baptism in the Holy Spirit right now. It's a matter of simply asking and receiving. Relax. God is good and He wants to give you good gifts. This is a safe place. There is no place for fear and no need for fear. He wants to fill you.'

What happened next still remains as vivid today as it was at that moment.

As Stuart prayed, asking the Holy Spirit to fill him, he began to feel what he describes as a 'bubbling sensation inside'. There was a burning within him too. He felt hot. He knew the Holy Spirit was filling him.

And the next moment, he was speaking in tongues. Arthur had explained that this was a common outworking of the baptism in the Holy Spirit – a language that was unlearned and given by God, and one that was so helpful in being able to praise and worship God. Tongues flowed that night.

Technicolour

It's hard to overstate this moment. That evening was life changing. Things have never been the same since. God did such a deep work in Stuart that night. It affected him deeply and it has had the most significant impact on all of his ministry. There was a new boldness about Stuart. He was less insecure in sharing his faith. When he read the Bible, the words meant more. The Holy Spirit was applying the Word to the reader in a new and powerful way.

Such was the overflow of the Holy Spirit in Stuart's life, for quite a while afterward he was concerned that he would burst out in speaking in tongues at an inappropriate moment. None more so than the very next day.

Stuart was on a day release from work, attending a local college to complete his Higher National Certificate. As the lecturer asked Stuart a question that day, it was hard to answer. There was such an overflow of the Holy Spirit, Stuart had to concentrate very hard in order to answer in English!

Life was suddenly on view in technicolour. Stuart could hear the Spirit speaking and prompting him in different situations. He found that he was being given the words to say as he ministered. He went about with a profound sense of the Spirit upon him, and this lasted for some weeks. When he slept, he sensed God's presence. When he woke, God was there with him. Looking back, Stuart considers those first few weeks of being filled as a time of being constantly aware of the Spirit's presence.

What followed was a voracious study of everything to do with the Holy Spirit. Books were purchased. Bible passages were studied. It was important to Stuart to steward what God had given. Even if the intensity of the experience dissipated, as it did over the weeks that followed, it was important to remain open to the Spirit, not to allow anything to interfere with listening to God, obeying Him, stepping out in ministry.

And stepping out in ministry was very much on God's agenda.

Chapter Two
The Advocates

John on lead guitar. Dave on rhythm guitar. Keith playing bass. And Stuart on keyboards. All four of them singing. Tight harmonies. Well-rehearsed.

It had to be. The early 1970s audiences could be tough. And there were a lot of people there that day.

The Miracle

Sligo. On the west coast of the Republic of Ireland. The band were there at the invitation of the Church Missionary Society.

It had been hard work to set up. To reach the stage they had to push through the crowds already arriving.

Later, peering out from the stage curtain, it was clear to Dave that more tickets had been sold than there were seats in the Town Hall.

'Guys, it's completely full! I'm not sure there's room for another person in there. Every seat is taken. They're filling the steps and the whole front of stage area.'

The evening goes well. People are appreciative, the applause is loud.

There's a problem with the props at one point. The helpers had put up a sign, each word painted onto single polystyrene tiles and stuck to the back wall of the stage: 'Go for Jesus!' Halfway through the second set, there is now so much perspiration in the hall due to the excessive numbers, it begins to affect the fixings on the wall. The tiles start to shift.

'Go' begins to slide to the ground, quickly followed by 'for', almost in time to the gentle song the band were singing.

John retrieves the situation.

'I want you to know that when all else fails, Jesus sticks!'

Laughter and applause and on with the set.

And then something happens.

At the end of the set, the band begin to sing 'Miracle'. It's the song they always finish with. And as always, it's the song they use to invite people to come forward to give their lives to Christ.

The problem is that tonight, there are far too many people in the venue to invite anyone forward.

As the band reaches the final verse, John begins to speak.

'It takes courage. It takes guts to do this. But if God has spoken to you this evening, if you are ready to give your life to Jesus Christ, I want to invite you to stay behind as we finish. Now is the time. Now is the time to say to all those around, "I'm going for this. I'm giving my life to Jesus Christ." Stay behind and we'll pray together.'

The song continues; Keith plays the melody on his guitar.

'Thank you for coming tonight. We appreciate the applause, but we want to give God the honour. It's to His glory that we do this. Thank you and good night.'

The band wait for the hall to clear in order to speak to those who want to give their lives to Jesus Christ.

The problem is, no one moves.

Stuart speaks.

'Thank you everyone. It's crowded in here tonight so can we ask that you leave as quickly as possible so we can speak to those who want to become Christians tonight.'

No one moves. The room is quiet.

Stuart coughs.

'So can I be clear, this is now just for those who want to be Christians tonight. For those who want to commit their lives to Jesus Christ. Maybe I can ask another way – do all of you here want to become Christians?

Then it happens. A low rumble, rising to a shout.

'Yes!'

Some are smiling. Some are in tears. The helpers from the Church Missionary Society are stuck to the spot. It's hard for them. They've not seen this before and have no idea what to do.

It's hard for the band too. Tears are just below the surface. This is why they do what they do. This is worth the long rehearsals, the hours of practice, the days – months – on the road.

All for Him.

Starting Out

Those early days in the Methodist Youth Group were the start of something much bigger. Not that Stuart knew that at the time. He and John led the occasional meeting and introduced some of the newer choruses beginning to arrive on the scene in the 1960s. The *Youth Praise* songbook was the go-to resource with one of the favourites being 'Can it be True?', a four-chord sequence easy to learn on the guitar and effective in worship.

By 1964 cousin Dave had joined John and Stuart, with Keith Howard making up the number. For a short while, they were also joined by a female vocalist, Lesley. All four boys had grown up together – the same primary and secondary schools, the same church, the same influences. And all four finding a faith in Christ at around the same time. Stuart and John were the younger two and had been in the same class, even sharing the same double desk at primary school.

It hadn't started that way. John recalls having Stuart in a headlock as he drove that same head towards a brick wall. A teacher intervened and insisted that the two become friends. They did.

Acoustic guitars and close harmonies were very much the order of the day for the newly formed band, with Stuart switching to keyboards once these could be afforded.

Initially, the band felt they were there simply to liven up the services. But it quickly became more than that. It became a lifesaver for the boys as well. The Methodist diet was a bit dry. Songs that expressed joy in worship were hard to come by. The band were well received, and the repertoire grew beyond covers of other bands' material through to writing their own songs. And as they wrote and performed, their own Christian faith grew too.

The band practised for hours. Songs were written and learned in each other's homes and then taken to a regular band practice at the West Parade Methodist Church building.

A small bio of the band, printed at a later date, records the official band debut as 5th May 1964. What started in the local youth group grew to include much of the county Methodist circuit. Ministers were grateful for the input into their youth groups and it wasn't long before the four were regularly travelling throughout Lincolnshire and beyond.

In those early days, a Christian band was something of a novelty. Young people were attracted to the concerts simply because they were so different from the rather formal meetings held in the church building on a Sunday. Extending their work into schools and singing in school assemblies was also unusual. Generally, the teachers welcomed the band and appreciated the message. The fact that the four by then had become so accomplished with their acoustic guitars and close harmonies added to the feeling that this was something special, something to be promoted.

Coffee-Bar Evangelism

'What do you think?'

The band were at one of their regular practices in the West Parade Methodist Church building. Having been asked to turn the volume down – a regular request! – the band were on a coffee break.

Dave was asking the question of the other three. The band had been together for a while now and further doors were beginning to open beyond the local Methodist circuit. Schools began to invite them in and with that, their music was getting known in other Christian streams and denominations. There was a sense of a call. As they prayed together, they were aware of God's invitation to preach the gospel through music.

So they needed a name.

'We're advocating the gospel, right?' said Dave. 'So how about "The Advocates"?'

And there it was. A band with a name.

The name was reflected into a later song called 'Here I Rest My Case':

Now it's over to you

Is all we've been saying true

Does it seem to make sense

Listening to the evidence?

We don't claim to have said

All there is to be said

But of one thing we are sure

Jesus will be all He claims to be and more

Here I rest my case. ©

The band were following a rich tradition of Christian bands in the latter half of the 1960s. Many had similar names. The Joystrings. The Overcomers. The Pilgrims. The Crossbeats. The Glorylanders.

Each of these bands had at least some impact on the newly formed Advocates, but it was secular music that most affected their sound. The increasingly searching lyrics of The Beatles linked with their simple harmonies went a long way to directing the early sound of The Advocates.

The young people of the day were looking for more than hymns and church services. It has always been thus. Every generation moves away from the one before it. It is a wise pastor who recognises this and does something positive with it, rather than trying to shut it down.

Coffee-bar evangelism was the result.

Most Friday nights in the middle to late 1960s, you could find the back halls of churches changed into coffee bars. Subdued lights. And as the 1970s arrived, maybe a psychedelic light show on the wall. Some form of constructed bar with bar stools. Soft drinks, coffee and tea.

And a band.

Not just on Friday evenings either. Often after the more formal Sunday evening gospel service across many churches in the UK, the back hall would be opened up for the youth.

Beyond this, a few commercial Christian coffee bars were established; the Mustard Seed in Sheffield and the Catacombs in Manchester being at the forefront. They would have bands playing live most nights, and The Advocates were regular performers.

Some of the bigger churches opened up their own coffee bars on the church premises as an ongoing concern, and again, these were populated by the up-and-coming Christian bands of the day.

A church in Colne, Lancashire, invited the band for a whole weekend. This was one of the first extended invitations and the band had to work hard to ensure they had enough material. This included extended preaching and testimonies. Dave remembers it as one of the first times that Stuart stepped out into a longer testimony, linked to teaching from the Bible.

The Colne invitation also required some serious thinking as to what to wear. Suits with black waistcoats and red ties became the distinctive visual of the band. They were copying their heroes The Beatles, as well as many other secular bands of the day such as The Mindbenders, The Dave Clark Five and The Kinks.

The intention was to communicate the Christian faith in a musical language that teenagers (itself a new word, coined less than ten years before) would understand. The music they chose to sing – increasingly their own material – was deliberately 'middle of the road'. This gave them access to the most venues and the widest audiences.

The band were successful. Not only in the quality of their sound but in the numbers coming to Christ at the end of their performances. They realised early on in their ministry that God was calling them primarily to evangelise and testimonies between songs became customary. The last song of the night was inevitably 'Miracle':

All that you need is a miracle

And all that you need can be yours

All that you need is available

The moment you turn to the Lord ©

As they sang, the tight harmonies soaring above the keyboards and the lead guitar, one of the band would speak over the song, inviting people to ask for a miracle that night, to come to the front, to invite Jesus into their lives.

And they did. In numbers. God was waking up a generation to the gospel and using the sounds of 1960s pop music to do so.

Not everyone was happy. One Christian leader of the day wrote a book condemning the move as being of the devil. But enough had the sense to see that the vehicle was not the problem and that without the attraction to the music of the day, many young people would never hear the gospel in the first place.

The band were sensitive to the criticism – one of their newsletter's records:

We realise that many of these things may bring criticism from our more conservative friends, but we believe that this is the way the Lord would have us go and the methods He would have us use to spread the gospel.

Open Doors

The man in the audience looked familiar. Stuart couldn't quite place him. He applauded enthusiastically throughout the set and stayed behind as the band counselled those who had responded to the invitation that evening.

'Hi, my name is Phil Vogel. I work with British Youth for Christ. I love what you were doing. It's a great sound and a clear message. Would you be interested in working with us?'

More open doors. Church youth groups, schools and larger gatherings. What started in the north and the Midlands was now right throughout the UK. It was pretty full-on for the four of them. Nearly every weekend was filled with concerts. Tours were arranged, at the expense of using up their holiday allowance from their jobs.

Phil became something of a father figure to the band, promoting them as associate evangelists for British Youth for Christ, and encouraging them on their journey.

Along the way, the equipment was improved and the move from entirely acoustic to electric achieved. A newsletter from July 1970 talks of the band acquiring 'a new uniform' to 'create a new image' along with the purchase of their own lighting. (Incidentally, the new uniform looked very much like the old uniform to this untrained eye.)

It was late one Saturday afternoon in February 1972, after a long rehearsal at West Parade and the band were back at Dave's house, in his study. They were praying about a forthcoming tour and Stuart spoke out in tongues. Dave gave the interpretation which had a prophetic element to it – primarily that it was time for the band to become full-time musicians. That God would provide. That they would travel to the four corners of the earth.

Keith responded. 'Do you think it's time? Should we do this full-time now? There are so many doors opening. I feel if we don't take this seriously, we may be missing what the Lord is saying to us. That interpretation seems clear enough to me.'

It wasn't a new discussion. The band had already raised the issue in the January 1972 newsletter with their supporters.

And it wasn't a long discussion either. The four band members knew each other well. They had worked through their differences. They understood the commitment.

It was time.

Validation

The Methodist church in Lincoln arranged for a valedictory service for the band in June that same year. The band's good friend Tony Stone was invited to speak. As he did so, he moved into prophecy.

History doesn't tell us what the Methodist leaders felt about a prophecy in their church building, but what is recorded is what Tony said. His prophecy was almost word for word the same as Dave's interpretation of Stuart speaking in tongues those few months earlier.

It was a strong confirmation for the band.

Notice given to their workplaces. Stuart and Dave to the council, John to his bank, Keith to the Civil Service. There was no going back now.

John on lead guitar. Dave on rhythm guitar. Keith playing bass. And Stuart on keyboards.

John managing the finance. Dave the administrator. Keith the main songwriter and arranger. And Stuart the pastor.

Already Stuart's pastoral gifts were being recognised and he became the one who managed the follow up, the prayer and the overall ministry.

July 1st, 1972. The full-time journey began.

Holy Spirit Days

These were heady days. The Holy Spirit was at work in a new and refreshing way across the UK, none more so than amongst church youth groups. Baptism in the Holy Spirit was being talked about and accepted – for the first time in a generation for some churches and denominations.

Across the Atlantic, a new Jesus Revolution was underway. Starting out on the West Coast of America, many young people were coming out of the hippie movement of the late 1960s and were finding faith in Christ. Unencumbered by expectations from established churches, they were breaking barriers in terms of sharing their faith in a relevant way, often including music that sounded very different from the formal hymns and choruses of the time.

At the head of this movement were singer-songwriters such as Larry Norman and Randy Stonehill. Close friends, both were recognisable by their long hair, jeans and t-shirts. And with many more following in their wake, both were soon in the UK, with concert tours arranged and LPs for sale.

In the UK, others were following the same lead. The Advocates found themselves working with fellow British Youth for Christ duo Ishmael & Andy. Malcolm & Alwyn were also on the scene. Like The Advocates, they were strongly influenced by The Beatles. Malcolm Wild and Alwyn Wall had actually met and been influenced by The Beatles in 1968 at a time when many were searching for the truth in Eastern religions. But both were to find the truth in Jesus Christ, resulting in a full-time music ministry in the UK.

It is quite possible that The Advocates were the first full-time Christian musicians of their generation though. Starting out in 1972 with a pretty full schedule, the work increased in 1973 and beyond. In total, they worked together as a band for eleven years, with seven of those in a full-time capacity. Their heart was simply to see people saved. Their passion was lives changed through Jesus Christ and the music was all towards that end. They were bold with the salvation message and were not afraid to go out onto the streets to seek an audience. The band had tracts regularly available, given out in the shopping centres along with a flyer for the concert that evening.

Living by Faith

The big challenge was income. The band were fully convinced of the call and also fully convinced that God would provide. They calculated that essential costs were around £10 a night for a concert plus 5p per mile for petrol – and that's what they said if asked. But they wouldn't ask themselves, trusting that whatever came in would be enough. Looking back, Stuart considers they were perhaps a little naïve in the approach they took.

There was a sense that God was on the case and that there would be no need to shout out for financial support – if He had called them to the task, then He would provide the money.

This approach is best demonstrated in their decision to buy sound equipment.

The band believed that God would provide the best sound equipment around and there was nothing better at the time than the HiWatt speakers and sound system. Along with Marshall, HiWatt were making a name for themselves for quality amplifiers. These were made by hand to a high spec by a small company in London, at that time working out of a garage.

The band had purchased the majority of their equipment. They had the suits too. Smart three-piece affairs now with the required big collars and flared trousers. Shoes always polished. A smart look. A professional look.

So the equipment needed to be professional too.

They were now in need of robust cabinets to fit the new speakers in. And they firmly believed that God would have them have the best. That meant HiWatt.

Having identified their needs, the order went in and the four musicians prayed and awaited God's provision.

The problem was that no money came in.

The deadline for collection and payment for the equipment was quickly approaching. Never mind, they reasoned, God is a God who often provides at the last minute. Let's keep praying and surely He will provide.

That was still the case as they drove down to London to collect the bespoke speaker cabinets on the due date.

It wasn't that God had not provided anything. They had most of the needed equipment. Dave's dad and his Hillman Minx had been the first source of transport, but God provided. Firstly, a green Bedford van, to which they adhered vinyl lettering spelling out the band's name. This van had to be abandoned, as recorded in one of their newsletters, due to 'suspension troubles, bad fumes . . . and general all-round deterioration'. The van they were now driving was a further testament to His faithfulness – a quality second-hand long-base Ford Transit. This would be the vehicle for most of the band's travels around the UK and into Europe.

Arriving at the garage where the equipment was made, the four were welcomed by the owner and shown the bespoke sound cabinets they had ordered.

'So that just leaves payment,' said the owner.

'Yes. About that. Has the money arrived yet?'

'What do you mean?'

'We're expecting the money to arrive with you today. I tell you what,' said Dave, 'it's still mid-morning. We'll go off and come back later in the day to check whether it's arrived.'

'No problem. See you later.'

The four of them found their way to a London park, parked up the van and began to walk and pray.

'Lord, we do feel you told us we should order the equipment. Please provide the money. Please send it through today.'

Expectations were high. They were even looking around at people passing them in the park, half expecting that someone would produce a brown envelope full of pound notes.

But nothing of the sort occurred.

'Do you think we've been a bit presumptuous? What if there is no money? What are we going to do?' said John.

Silence.

And a growing realisation that they might just have been carried along on a rather naïve expectation that wasn't entirely based on a good understanding of how God usually provides. Sure, there were such stories, and reading the biographies of the day such as Corrie Ten Boom and Richard Wurmbrand, the band had a similar expectation. But there was a bit of a difference. The two books mentioned both reflected a time of severe persecution, one in the war and one behind the Iron Curtain of Communism. Maybe God didn't always answer that way. Maybe they should have asked friends and family to help them. Maybe they'd got this a little bit the wrong way around.

In the end the band felt that the only thing they could do was tell the truth to the business owner. Dave was the de-facto leader of the group at that time so he was volunteered to talk to the owner.

'Hi, has the money arrived?'

'No, nothing's come in.'

'Oh. Okay. Well, this may appear a bit strange to you but we are a Christian band and we expected that the money would be provided by God for us to buy the equipment. We still do feel that, but obviously it's not there yet.'

'That's okay,' said the man. 'Give me a call when the money's arrived and you can come down and collect it. I'll keep it for you.'

A chastened group of friends made their way back up the motorway, grateful for the man's understanding and willingness to wait, along with some earnest prayers as to what they were meant to do.

They started with their own bank accounts, figuring that they couldn't ask others to give sacrificially where they had not first given themselves.

It wasn't long afterwards that the band were able to make the return journey to London, cash in hand. It hadn't taken long for friends and family to respond to the need, and the new equipment came back up the motorway that day with four young men having learned a few lessons about stepping out in faith.

Throughout their time as a full-time band, they never charged for their concerts. They made their needs known to hosts and to supporters if asked, and trusted that God would do the rest.

He did.

At times it was a bit 'hand to mouth' in terms of income, but they were never without provision.

The band would assess their needs on a monthly basis and check their bank account at the end of each month to make sure it was still in the black.

One month the band were owed an amount of £235.86. It hadn't arrived within the expected timescale and the money was genuinely needed by the band to cover living costs. John went into the bank to find out how much was available and could be withdrawn in lieu of the outstanding figure.

He came out of the bank with an amount of money and the widest of grins.

'You know we're owed £235.86? Guess how much was in our account . . . £235.86!'

Chapter three
THE JOURNEY

There is no doubt that as 1972 morphed into 1973, The Advocates were one of the biggest of the UK Christian bands around. And they were on a journey that was to take them well beyond Lincolnshire – and well beyond the shores of the United Kingdom.

Now with their van and their new equipment, the professionalism was apparent. The quality of the sound was significantly improved as well.

Stuart had expanded his own sound too. The band's newsletter of January 1972 records the replacement of the old keyboard with a new 'Jennings three-manual organ' with the top keyboard (of three) acting as a soundalike for a harpsichord or xylophone.

The suits were still on view, along with the waistcoats, but now with open neck shirts and longish hair in the required revised Beatles style of the day.

Working Men's Clubs
The links with British Youth for Christ had brought the band to the attention of a wider audience and this led to further concerts outside of the usual Christian scene, including the Army barracks

in Belfast, churches of all denominations throughout Ireland, and concerts in prisons. Plus, a growing number of working men's clubs back in England.

Most of these clubs were found in the north of the country and were therefore on the doorstep for the band. It was a brave thing to say 'yes'. The atmosphere in these clubs was very different from the Christian coffee bars. Youngers Tartan, Watney's Red and Double Diamond were not the names of other groups but of the beers of the day, freely flowing throughout the evening.

Often the band would be given a Sunday night slot, following on from a blue comedian, which made it even more interesting. Filled with cigarette smoke, there was no need for any smoke effects in the performances. Shouting and barracking was common and the only response was to turn the volume up on the speakers.

Clapp's Café is a venue the band remember to this day. One of the roughest venues they ever sang at, the café was near Tiverton in Devon. The band were playing because of a cancellation from a secular group who had refused to perform due to the amount of aggression received from the audience at an earlier concert. The audience were a mix of local working men and young people who had had too much to drink. With the swearing and the spitting, it was hard to keep going that night and the band had to resort to increasing the volume considerably more than usual to get to the end of the set!

A Baptist church in Newark was another challenging moment with Keith being pushed around by a gang of Hells Angels who decided to invade the premises.

Open responses to Christ were less common at the working men's clubs but there is no doubt that many men did respond, whether openly or quietly in their own time. Hardened drinkers used to a full physical workout in the factories were challenged with a spiritual workout and found the answer in Jesus Christ.

It's clear that the band were both bold in their proclamation of the gospel – not for them the reflective hippie vibe of the day with songs that may or may not speak of spirituality – and with their complete lack of fear in singing in challenging atmospheres. None more so than one time in Exeter. Their local organiser had heard that a secular band had pulled out from being the support act before the new Jimi Hendrix film was shown at the local theatre. The Advocates got the gig. It was there that a young man came onto the stage in mid performance to declare that he was the Messiah. Unabashed, the band turned the volume up and continued.

Another time saw the band performing at the Web Coffee Bar in Northampton to a hostile audience. Their newsletter records:

> We pushed our equipment along a stone floor, set up amidst the paint tins, but played despite the competition of a football machine. This was a very difficult evening but made us re-examine our attitude and approach towards difficult audiences.

Audiences were occasionally difficult for another reason. A concert with Malcolm & Alwyn in Sutton-in-Ashfield was interrupted by a protest – a group of Christians denouncing the musicians and declaring the music as 'satanic'.

Big Moments

The profile of the group within the Christian scene in the UK was growing further. British Youth for Christ events throughout the nation led to more bookings and ever higher profile events. In fact one of the confirmations of the band's resolution to become full-time musicians was a full calendar within weeks of that decision.

Trips to Ireland became more frequent, working with churches in both the north and south of Ireland, supported with specific prayer meetings back in the UK. Some events were deliberately promoted by Catholic and Protestant churches together. At one concert, the appeal at the end of the meeting saw a number of Catholic priests respond. Precious moments and such a thrill for the band to see the Holy Spirit at work in such a way.

Concerts in the soldiers' barracks were particularly memorable at a time of increased troubles in the city of Belfast. A Sergeant Major confided in the band that at some time or another he had seen practically every man in his battalion get down on their knees and pray. The ferocity of the riots and fighting at that time meant that the men didn't know whether they were going to come back from patrol duty.

University work opened up, especially working with a young Roger Forster (later the leader of the Ichthus church movement) as he pioneered gospel events across campuses. Schools work continued too, with one of the early Advocates newsletters celebrating twenty-seven young ladies coming to Christ at Boston Girls' High School.

At one point, concept concerts became a thing – setting each half of the evening around a theme such as the fall of man followed by Christ's redemption. The songs were occasionally linked by classical music and narration and supported with slides and lighting changes.

Possibly the strangest booking of all was as competitors in the 'Miss Disco Girl' pop bands competition in Peterborough. The event was being judged by Radio One DJ Ed Stewart in front of an audience of around 900 youngsters . . . they didn't win.

Platforms were often shared with other Christian musicians of the day, including Malcolm & Alwyn, Lois Buckley, Garth Hewitt and Graham Kendrick – and one of the more unusual performers, the Ralph Chambers Number One Mobile Gospel Disco!

Buzz Magazine was the voice of the young church in the 1970s and they were keen to interview The Advocates. The band then appeared at a large Christian concert organised by the magazine, and later a concert at the Royal Albert Hall sponsored by the YMCA.

The Billy Graham Association began to invite the band to their events and, as a result, The Advocates found themselves on the stage at Spree 73, a celebration at Earls Court with 22,000 in attendance. Inspired by America's Christian youth event Explo '72, the Billy Graham Association were keen to reach British youth with the gospel and invited bands and singers to join them. The band found they were sharing the bill with Cliff Richard and Jonny Cash among others. This in turn led to another Billy Graham Association event in Europe. Eurofest '75 gathered similar numbers in Brussels.

Interestingly, at the time The Advocates were the only 'electric' band the Billy Graham Association were willing to work with in the UK.

1973 also saw the band recording their first LP on the newly created Dovetail label, managed by Musical Gospel Outreach, the company behind *Buzz Magazine*. The band were provided with session musicians to help fill the sound – particularly drums as, rather unusually, the band were entirely guitar and keyboards based.

Called *The Advocates*, the very first release for Dovetail, labelled *Dovetail 1*, it sold well, and the reviews were good, including this one from Ken Scott:

This British pop-rocking male foursome delivers a fine debut full of hooks and melodies. Lively presentation, catchy tunes, bold harmonies, invigorated with a crisp electric guitar presence. Lots of organ too, which gives the album more of a 60s sound with flashbacks to the whole British Invasion thing. I'm usually not a fan of horns, but here they're used to good effect, as on their energetic arrangement of 'Rise, Shine'. They get down into some loud boogie-style rock-and-roll on 'No Man's Land' and 'Jumpin' Jeremiah', both of which have blazing guitar solos. 'Alive' rocks pretty heavily as well, while 'Revolution' marches sturdily along in 60s garage-band fashion.

The self-titled album was followed up with a John Pantry produced sound in 1975, *Here I Rest My Case*. Recorded in August and September the previous year, this was more of a concept album (popular in its day) with songs taking the listener through the claims of Christ. It received a very positive review in *Buzz Magazine* and an extremely negative one in *The Methodist Recorder*. This suggests the band were reaching their target audience.

Despite the albums and the higher profile, the band were most at ease in the coffee bars and pubs; smaller venues with an intimate atmosphere that allowed them to share testimony in a way that resulted in many young people finding a faith in Christ.

One of the boldest ventures was a six-week tour of Europe, soon after going full time. Starting in the Netherlands at the invitation of the Dutch Youth for Christ, the band travelled in their Ford Transit over thousands of miles, sleeping wherever accommodation was offered – and when it was not, on top of the equipment in the back of the van.

Days were spent with Youth for Christ staff on the streets of the towns, sometimes sitting in a circle on the pavements and 'singing choruses' as they describe it in their newsletter. Off the back of this, someone would speak for a few minutes and flyers were then distributed for the concert that evening.

One of the more unusual results of the Dutch tour was the formation of 'The Little Advocates', two girls aged eleven and eight, who translated the band's songs into Dutch and sang at a number of venues.

With hindsight, the tour was too long. Bearing in mind Stuart and Irene were married at this stage and with Andrew their firstborn, it wasn't the kind of schedule that fostered a happy marriage. All of the band felt the strain of such a long tour and agreed they would limit their time away from home to a maximum of seven days in the future.

The Canadian Risk

Other European adventures followed as well as one of the highlights of the years in the band – a trip to Canada.

Plans had started well for this big adventure. A friend of British Youth for Christ was the main contact. There was a genuine excitement with this opportunity and the band prepared as well as they could. Dates were agreed for a month's tour in June 1973.

It all came crashing down when a telegram arrived in February of that year.

I'm sorry to say I have been unable to make any firm bookings. Churches and youth groups are advising that they have not heard of The Advocates and that as they are not a known quantity in Canada, they are unwilling to

52

make any commitment to a tour. My apologies. I suggest we cancel.

That evening the band gathered to pray. The conclusion of that time was a feeling that they should still go. But how? No local organiser. No pre-publicity. No firm commitments. It was a significant risk on a number of fronts.

Then came the telegram: 'Nothing working. Still coming?'

'Guys, I think we need to ask God for confirmation on this one.' The voice was Dave's, but it was what all four were feeling. They prayed again.

Yes, they still felt to go. Their reply telegram said, 'Still coming. Don't worry. Just trust.'

The very next day, a letter arrived with a Building Society cheque and an anonymous scrappy note attached which simply said, 'For air fares.'

The thing is nobody knew of the Canada trip. The band had not made it public. In Europe, they travelled by road using the van. They had no need for air fares, except for that one possibility. Canada.

Six tickets for Canada. The four band members plus Stuart's wife Irene and Dave's wife Janetta. Four acoustic guitars and a pile of luggage.

No bookings.

On arrival in Vancouver, the original contact was kind enough to pick them up. The band went to the local old people's homes and started that way. Playing, sharing, praying. This brought about a contact with the Mennonite church movement in Canada. At the end of two weeks, the band were asked to sing at the Mennonite Youth Camp at Camp Squeah, way up in the Rocky Mountains, near the town of Hope. This was becoming quite the adventure.

The engagements started to come in at that point and the band decided to accept one in the town of North Battleford. This was just short of a 1000-mile journey through the Rocky Mountains from Vancouver.

A car was needed. But the hire companies were not interested. The band were self-employed so there could be no employer reference and a large deposit was not a possibility. In the end, a lady from Hertz came to the rescue:

'I'm an atheist, but I trust Christians. I'll let you have a vehicle.'

And what a vehicle. A big Lincoln Continental. Three in the front. Three in the back. And room for the guitars.

As the finance man, John remembers that the offering they received at the end of the Mennonite Youth Camp provided for their hire costs and fuel to within two dollars of the actual cost.

Upon arrival in North Battleford, the band found out that the Hertz dealership had closed a couple of years before. The local garage sorted it out for them.

So just to be clear. They hired a car they should not have been able to hire, without the required paperwork and without a financial guarantee. They then drove to a place where the dealership was no longer active. And when they did the maths, the offering from Camp Squeah matched the hire and petrol costs almost exactly.

Faith lesson learned.

God is No Man's Debtor

North Battleford happened to be celebrating that week, reflecting back to the early European settlers who had arrived in the 1870s. Consequently, the band were adopted by the town! Concerts followed in a number of the schools, one for the Canadian Mounted Police and, of course, in numerous churches. One concert in a village outside the town saw three young girls come to Christ. It might have been passed over in any recollection of Stuart's life, except for the fact that one of the girls married a well-known Bible College professor later in life who together had a significant effect on the Canadian Church – a story picked up on by the band's old friend Tony Stone some years later. Interestingly, years later Stuart discovered that North Battleford had been the starting place for the Latter Rain movement, which was a prophetic prayer movement influencing the later Charismatic renewal.

As the journey came to an end and the band were driven to the airport, they calculated that they were around $100 short in order to pay final costs. They were grateful for the significant and miraculous gifts that had been received for the tour but concerned that they were still short on cash.

The driver called in to his church on the way to the airport. An envelope had been left for the band. In it was $100.

Decisions made in faith in the UK with money miraculously given. Twenty-seven engagements on a four-week trip with no prior bookings. All costs met. And numerous lives changed as a result.

There is one final postscript to this particular tour. Years later Stuart met up with the couple who had sent the anonymous cheque through the post for the air fares. At the time, they had been planning to marry but felt they were to give all their savings to the band. They were obedient. By the time of their marriage, so much money had flowed back into their bank account from various sources, they were able to buy a five-bedroomed house.

Hebrews 6:10 in the Bible says, 'God is not unjust so as to overlook your work and the love that you have shown for his name in serving the saints.' A loose translation – God is no man's debtor.

On the Road

The band were always ready to accept whatever accommodation was offered when they were on the road. It became a bit of a standing joke that Stuart always seemed to manage the poorest offered accommodation. One time, near Northampton, he was sleeping in a conservatory on an air bed that kept deflating through the night while Dave, who had been taken down the road to the house of another congregation member, managed a double bed with an en-suite.

On a trip to Rotterdam, Stuart had had such a bad run of poor accommodation compared to the other band members, he announced that he was going to be the first in line for accommodation that night. Dave drove the band around to different congregation members that evening and as soon as he pulled up at the first house, Stuart was out of the car, announcing that he was taking first choice.

What Stuart didn't see – and the other band members did – was a man in the window looking out at them, dressed in a coat, scarf and hat. Bearing in mind this was a warm summer night, it looked rather odd to say the least.

Stuart was shown upstairs to his bed for the night. The lady hosting him only spoke a little English, but enough to explain that Stuart was sleeping on a mattress up a ladder in the loft. The room was not much larger than a coffin, and when the door was closed the loft was almost airtight. Things took an even more bizarre turn the next day when the man in the coat (still wearing it) turned up at the dinner table and proceeded to spit into a bucket throughout the meal.

The other band members? Each had a good night's sleep in real beds with a welcoming host.

Stuart did seem to be the subject not just of poor accommodation but of a number of pranks. The band newsletter for July 1971 records a sightseeing trip to a reservoir where 'Stu's feet suddenly decided to go for a swim, quite against his will. Stu didn't really appreciate it, but we certainly did.'

Smuggled Bibles

The Advocates made numerous trips to the Netherlands, where Youth for Christ were particularly strong, then later into Finland, Belgium, Austria and Germany. The German tour was especially interesting as the band were able to travel through into East Germany, behind the Iron Curtain.

In an age before the World Wide Web, Bibles in the Communist Bloc were hard to come by, so the band took a number of boxes of Bibles with them in the van. They decided that rather than hide them, they would put the boxes in plain view.

When the customs officials inspected the van at the border, they were very thorough. Mirrors underneath the van, sniffer dogs, an inspection of the equipment. All thoroughly examined. Except for the boxes of Bibles. They remained in full view in the back of the van. And they remained unopened!

On arriving with their host church in East Germany, the band were told that the local authorities had banned the concert from being held in the church building. Unperturbed, the local congregation simply hired a community hall and the concert went ahead.

It was a difficult journey through East Germany, not least because the band were clearly being followed. A couple of gentlemen in dark raincoats – even looking like spies – followed them everywhere.

The early European concerts had been the catalyst for the band going into full-time ministry. The stress of the later tours was the catalyst for the band considering that the time had come to pack away the amps and speakers and seek God for whatever was next for each of them.

Final Concert

The band's final major concert was sponsored by Musical Gospel Outreach. With a wide variety of artists, The Advocates sang for one last time at the Royal Albert Hall on 10th January 1976 in an event called *Welcome to the Family*. By then John was becoming increasingly involved with Youth for Christ missions and later with Bob Gordon Ministries. Dave and Keith were still home-based and supporting Stuart as they started to work out what to do with the numbers of young people finding a faith in Christ but not finding a home in church.

One of the artefacts from those heady days is a schedule for the years 1973 to 1975. This documents each concert, numbers counselled and decisions made. If this spreadsheet could speak it would be shouting 'hallelujah' as it records a three-year attendance of around 270,000 with over 2,000 young people praying a prayer to ask Jesus into their lives. 1,226 bookings over three years. 300 concerts, 200 church services, nearly 100 coffee bars and 200 schools. 37 rallies, 44 concerts to soldiers, 87 days travelling, 632 days working. Lives changed forever.

What a journey. A generation impacted by four young men unashamedly preaching Christ.

Chapter Four
Church By Accident

Past 11.00pm on a Friday night. The doorbell rings.

Stuart and Irene look at each other quizzically. On with the dressing gown and down the stairs.

It's Katherine. One of the girls who has recently found faith. She had been at the house earlier in the evening for the informal Bible studies Stuart and Irene had been running, with the help of other Advocates band members.

'I'm so sorry it's this late,' says Katherine, 'but I found these two guys on the way home.'

Two rather dishevelled characters move out of the shadows and appear in the doorway. The smell of alcohol is the first thing Stuart notices.

'I didn't know what to do so I brought them to you.'

The gas fire in the lounge is relit and cups of coffee are offered.

Neither were in a suitable condition for much conversation. One of them proceeded to be sick and after a short while both left with information about an evangelistic meeting that was soon taking place. To Stuart and Irene's surprise, around twelve young men arrived at this meeting, though it appeared that their main intent was to disrupt proceedings. At the close of the meeting, one of the two who had turned up at the house received Christ. In a wonderful turnaround, that man, Dave, is now married to Stuart's sister Elizabeth and together they lead a church in Skegness.

Such encounters were not uncommon. Hard to deal with, but a growing part of Stuart and Irene's early married life as God began to move in a powerful way among the young people in Lincoln and beyond.

Bridging the Gap

The Methodist Church were supportive of the work The Advocates were doing and had sponsored the band to go into schools in the Lincoln area for a week of evangelism. The school concerts were supported by further evening meetings at various churches.

The events were a success. Many young people prayed with the band and asked Jesus to change their lives.

The problem came with what to do next. The band took the young people through the *Journey into Life* booklet, a popular introduction to the Christian faith . . . But then what? They tried taking the young people along to church on Sunday, but there was no denying that their experience there was nowhere near the same level as at the concerts. Most of the young people found it difficult to follow the services and were uncomfortable with the formality.

Maybe the answer was a church outside of formal church? As the band announced to their supporters the beginning of the end for The Advocates, that same newsletter from October 1975 records:

From the mission we took part in last November [in Lincoln], a number of young people became Christians and since then it has become increasingly apparent that there is a need to cater for young people with very little church background.

Stuart asked the minister at West Parade Methodists whether it would be possible to use the vestry on a Monday night for a more informal meeting. Permission was granted and, without knowing it at the time, the start of a new church had begun.

It wasn't long afterwards that another move was agreed. The minister's vestry on a Monday night wasn't ideal. With hard chairs, a damp atmosphere and smelling of old hymn books with overtones of duplicator fluid from the Banda machine, it wasn't exactly conducive to meeting together informally. With the leaders' agreement, the move was made to Stuart and Irene's house on a Friday night.

Marriage

Stuart and Irene had not long been married. A nervous bride and groom exchanged rings on 3rd April 1972, in front of a full church at West Parade. It had been a particularly windy morning, with guests having been blown in for an 11.00am wedding. The ladies of the church arranged for a salad lunch in the church hall afterwards.

Stuart and Irene had met four years earlier.

Having moved from Hull, Irene's family were welcomed into the West Parade church, not least by Stuart's mum and dad. It wasn't long before Irene and her sister Ann were calling round at the house and getting to know Stuart and Graham, and younger sister Elizabeth. And it wasn't long either before Stuart was paying a little more attention to Irene.

'Irene, I'm going to the water festival in Lincoln on Saturday, do you fancy meeting up?' delivered with a calmness that Stuart wasn't particularly feeling. He breathed a sigh of relief when Irene said 'yes'.

May 4th, 1968 at the water festival. Irene remembers the exact date. Stuart does too with a bit of help – by identifying that this was the day of the FA Cup final!

It really was love at first sight. Stuart was still in the sixth form at the City School and Irene was by then a dental nurse. He was careful when meeting Irene after school to take the tie off and hide the school cap in his pocket!

Irene joined in with the band activities, already becoming well known in 1968, by helping at events.

Money was 'limited' (Stuart's understated description of being broke), so by the time of the wedding, there wasn't much left. The honeymoon was in the flat of a friend in Scarborough. But a limited honeymoon spend meant that they had been able to afford a mortgage and the young couple moved into a terraced house in Richmond Road on their return, costing the princely sum of £2,500.

Andrew arrived in 1973, and with the band at its height, Stuart regrets not being at home so much in Andrew's early years. Rebekah arrived three years later. Dave is very much the baby of the family, putting in an appearance a decade later.

Their good friend Jeff Lucas observes of the marriage that in their ministry together they are the perfect partnership, with Irene's eye for detail, humour and welcome complementing Stuart's gentle determination. In Jeff's words when considering their service to God, 'They mean it.'

Chris Bowater, another close friend over the years, recognises that same 'they mean it' trait when applied to the Church. Stuart has a well-developed sense of what 'ecclesia' should be – he has a vision for what the Church is and what it can do in the world today. This passion for Church is reflected in everything Stuart and Irene were to attempt in the years to come.

Even knocking down walls.

Knocking Down Walls

'We really are going to have to do something!'

Stuart and Irene are talking over coffee on a Saturday morning, having had over thirty young people in their home the night before. Filling the lounge and travelling up the hallway and stairs on a Friday night, the decision was taken to knock down a wall. There was a builder living just over the road who was able to help at a comparatively low cost.

The decision to knock a wall down is reflective of a couple entirely committed to all that God would have them do. The meetings needed to happen. There was nowhere else suitable. So it had to happen.

Dave and Keith from the band were often with Stuart and Irene in these meetings – John was working away with Youth for Christ by now. Keith was a particularly accomplished musician and was often the one to lead worship with his guitar.

There were some wonderful new sounds around at that time. *Youth Praise* had been ditched and new songs were coming out from some of the early days of the house church movement and the Bible Week gatherings that took place in the summer months. *Songs of Fellowship,* a songbook accompanied by worship albums, became an extremely successful resource and introduced many churches to a new era of God-orientated worship. Lyrics centred on who God was and what He had done through Christ. Worshippers were caught up in expressing the grandeur of God and all He had accomplished for each one, adding a personal and reflective emphasis to worship. Such a change of emphasis from the extremely dry 'hymn sandwiches' of formal denominational church meetings.

House Church

The meetings were a success. In fact, it wasn't so much meetings as lifestyle. Stuart and Irene opened their home and young people would regularly appear on the doorstep at odd times of the day and night. The house became a centre for fun and friendship, all of it around clear Bible teaching and refreshing worship. Some even moved in for a while on a modest rent.

The early 1970s saw the growth of a new phenomenon in the UK – the establishing of house churches. One of the early pioneers, Gerald Coates, had been shown the left boot of fellowship from the Brethren Church and ended up by default with one of the first house churches in the country, based in Cobham.

House church was the obvious route to go, especially as the established Methodist church were struggling as to what to do with Stuart and Irene and their growing numbers. Stuart had asked whether there could be an affiliation with the Methodist Church denomination and even spoke to some senior people in the district about it, but the answer was a polite 'no'. The concept was too far away from what the Methodists understood as church in those days, so in the end they reached an amicable separation. To this day Stuart and Irene remain extremely grateful to the Methodist Church – especially the local congregation at West

Parade – for their early support and long-suffering management of what became an extremely excited and noisy youth movement.

The final decision came by way of a prophecy from Dave Kitchen. In it, he spoke of God's heart for the young people and that they should start a church in the north of the city – it was that specific. The prophetic word aligned with what others were thinking, and with the separation from the Methodists, the way forward became clear.

Wilmin Hall

'We're starting on Sundays. We'll still carry on with Friday nights round our place, but we feel that God is growing us into a church. We've hired Wilmin Hall. Please join us there!'

The announcement on that Friday night was not unexpected. The group had been growing and a number of the older generation had expressed an interest in joining – local people who were looking for more than their Methodist and Brethren assemblies could offer. Plus Stuart and Irene's parents. Dave's dad was there as well. Young families too. This was beginning to look a lot more generational. A lot more like Church.

And here we see Stuart the decision-maker. He wasn't afraid to make the big call when it was needed. But always in the context of working with others and seeking the views of others. Band member John recalls observing this approach on numerous occasions in those early days, and the mix of boldness and collaboration has served Stuart well over the years.

Wilmin Hall was an old wooden hut to the north of the city. Cheap to hire and in possession of an ancient wood burner to keep its occupants warm, it was pretty basic. But just what was needed as Stuart and Irene stepped out on this new adventure. Keith was still with them, but by now Dave was away working with the Don Summers Crusade and John had relocated to Norwich.

Despite the concern for not complicating church life, fairly early on in the journey there was a need for a bank account. And for a bank account you needed a name and a charitable trust.

The debate wasn't a long one. Stuart and Irene talked with their fellow leaders, which by this stage included Stuart's dad.

'We want to represent Lincoln, so that has to be in the title. And we want to be free in the Holy Spirit. So how about Lincoln Free Church?'

And there it was. The beginning of another journey.

Full Time

It wasn't long before the church had to move again, this time to Newport Hall, an old Baptist building not far away. This move in 1978 was significant in another way – the church bought the building. This itself was quite something – most of the church were still young but between them they were able to find the £15,000 needed.

Just a line in a book. But £15,000 in those days represented sacrifice. Members sold cars, furniture, tithed and double-tithed. This was an exciting adventure. God was blessing them. They were growing. They were reaching their community. A reflection of a burgeoning new church movement in the UK, these were heady days.

The amount paid for the building came about in an unusual manner. The seller was asking for one amount and the church were offering a lower figure. Dave Kitchen felt that the church should have a gift day and that whatever the total amount was, this should be the amount offered. That's a bit of a risk of course, but the leaders felt it was the way to go. Including money in the bank, the total came to £15,000. Which happened to be halfway between the asking price and the original offer price.

Initially with the band, Stuart had been full time in ministry for some years by now. In fact, he never really went back to traditional employment from his days in The Advocates.

He did need to make ends meet though and this was accomplished in a rather unique way for a while. Stuart went along to the local meat factory.

'Hello, I'm a local minister. I'd like to take a part-time job. Is there anything you can accommodate me with?'

The lady behind the desk looked a bit nonplussed.

'Er . . . What do you mean?'

'A job. Do you have any part-time work?'

'To be honest, as a church minister I think you may be a little overqualified.'

It took a while for Stuart to persuade the local manager that he was serious but, sure enough, he was taken on as a meat packer. He worked on the potted meat machine and stacking hams in fridges, 6.00am until 8.00am every weekday. It was a rough place. On one occasion Stuart was locked in the ice room during the tea break, but he pretended nothing had happened and went on working. It brought him a certain amount of respect with the rest of the workforce, who would regularly refer to him as 'the vicar'.

For Stuart growing up, a minister of religion was a vicar without O Levels, but he was learning fast. He embarked on a Certificate of Ordination, qualifying through the ministry of evangelism with an ordination service in an Elim church in Birmingham in 1977. By 1980, working through correspondence courses, he had added a certificate from Australia's Central School of Religion and a Batchelor of Theology degree with Divinity College, Florida.

Back to Acts

Acts of the Apostles had been a key book back in the days when the church met in Stuart and Irene's home. It was studied in depth, with a longing that, as they grew as a church, they would emulate those early apostles as far as possible. Structure for structure's sake was avoided. Relationships were key. Growth was among friends and friends of friends, with regular numbers finding a faith in Christ – in the early years through The Advocates and later directly through outreach and open-house meetings.

Steps of faith as a church were often taken in prayer with a binding of enemy activity and loosing of all that God intended. Stuart and Dave had been particularly taken by a magazine article in *Revival*, a Crusade for World Revival publication. The January 1979 edition included a piece by Derek Prince, explaining the principle of binding the enemy in prayer.

The meetings themselves were both Sunday morning and Sunday evening with smaller house groups in the week. The Sunday evening meetings were less structured – and long! People would share what they felt God was saying. There would be room for testimony, prophecy, praying together, healing and more. Having their own building meant there was no particular time to shut up shop and this was reflected in some meetings closing as late as 11.00pm.

The unstructured meetings did have their downside. Stuart had to deal on a number of occasions with strange visions along the lines of 'I see a potato; I don't know what it means . . .' There was a willingness to put up with a lot simply because they were family together. Stuart recalls the violin player who brought his own unique style of accompaniment. But they loved people and gave as much freedom as possible.

Family Together

This was church family. Everyone in it together, building church in a new way.

Stuart and Irene's older children, Andrew and Becki, remember those times at church. They weren't always the best behaved during the sermon and on more than one occasion were removed by Irene for laughing too loud at inappropriate moments.

Those early days as a church were particularly precious. Set free from the rigidity of denominations, the church found a new love for Christ. There was a passion in the worship and a compassion for the city. Leading was easy. There didn't seem to be any arguments. No gossip or backbiting. A freshness in relationships reflecting a freshness in the Holy Spirit.

Andrew recalls being concerned if he missed a meeting: 'There were so many exciting things happening, you just didn't want to miss out.'

Fun times too. There would be church-wide football matches, reflecting Stuart's love of the game. Matches with other congregations too – including the infamous one where Stuart received a severe gash on his leg. Andrew and Becki remember the blood. Stuart remembers the match, playing on through the injury – and winning!

The majority of the congregation would go to the local park after the Sunday morning meetings, with picnics through the summer months when the weather would allow. For the children, everyone was called 'auntie' or 'uncle' even though they weren't.

As the 1970s rolled into the 1980s, the new church phenomena continued to grow at pace, and Newport Hall was at the forefront of that move, particularly as regards to Lincoln and the surrounding area.

Lenchwood

'We're planning a weekend away – we hope as many of you as possible can come.'

With the dates announced, most of the church planned to be there. Lenchwood. A Christian Centre in the Vale of Evesham. Eddie Smith, a Christian minister who had been helping with the Lincoln church, was the speaker.

That first Saturday was wet. People had managed to get their tents up in the dry but were grateful that the meetings themselves were in the main centre.

That night, Stuart is wide awake. At the end of the meeting, he decides to go for a walk and is joined by eight other friends. Irene stays behind in the caravan, looking after Andrew and Becki.

The ground is soaking, so Stuart has his walking boots on. It's getting colder too. He asks to borrow an Aran sweater from his father-in-law.

With the rain clouds dispersed, the evening is rather lovely by now. Stuart and friends continue to chat together about the day as they walk down the field.

Then it happens. As they step over a line in the field, the ground appears to be warm.

'That's really strange,' says one of the party. The whole group of them test out the finding, stepping back over the line into the colder air, and then back again onto the warm ground.

There is no doubt about it, there is something happening that has warmed the ground. They try and work out why. Maybe it's some pipes in the soil.

'I don't know,' says someone, 'but can't you just feel God here too?'

The next thing any of the nine friends remember is being on the ground. All nine have fallen to the floor at the same moment, with an incredible sense of God's presence. Overwhelmed by what they are feeling, they lie there, looking up at the stars. What feels like a few minutes turns into nearly three hours.

Three hours in God's presence, lying on warm ground in the middle of a field.

Eventually, all nine sense that whatever it is that God was doing has passed and they return to the campsite.

The next day Stuart raises it with Eddie Smith. Eddie is a bit sceptical. He puts it down to youthful enthusiasm and, with that, the Sunday meetings progress. What Eddie didn't know was that his own wife went for a walk that morning with one of the site owners, an elderly lady in her eighties. As the two women walk down the field, they too fall to the floor. Stuart happens to look up at that moment and witnesses them falling.

Now Eddie is a convert. He seeks out the two elderly ladies who manage Lenchwood and asks some questions. As a result, they pull out some old maps, and there on the site, at the exact point where the warm earth was, are the markings of an old monastery. Further investigation identifies that the monks at this particular monastery had prayed regularly for revival.

It never happened again. The church returned the year after but there was no warm earth, no falling to the floor.

That night, as Stuart returned to his caravan at 1.30 in the morning, he tried not to wake Irene and the children. Taking off his boots, he noticed his socks were soaking wet from all the rain on the field. Fearing the worst for the white Aran sweater he'd borrowed from his father-in-law, he gingerly removed it. It was dry. More than that, there wasn't a single mark or stain on it. Proof, if it were needed, that the ground really was warm that night.

What does it all mean? It's probably best not to dig too deeply into creating a revival theology around it. But simply to acknowledge that on a starry night in the summer of 1980 God met with Stuart and a number of his church in a field in the Vale of Evesham. In the same place that many had prayed for revival in earlier centuries.

Today that same location is used for David's Tent, an annual 72-hour non-stop worship event where thousands come away to worship Jesus together.

Chapter Five
The Vision And The Call

A nine-year-old boy sits quietly in the church pew. The Methodist minister is part way through his sermon, but the boy is listening to a different voice.

It was then that Stuart knew God had a special plan for his life. Even at nine, there was an awareness of more, a sense that God's hand was on his life. It would be a few years later, at the age of fourteen, before Stuart would find a certainty in his Christian faith but, to be honest, there was never a time when he was unaware of God.

His early influences were Bible teachers. His dad for a start. Those reel-to-reel tapes from Francis Dixon. Copious numbers of David Pawson teaching cassettes played in the van when travelling with The Advocates. Then the more formal qualifications from his links with Bible colleges. All this has produced a Christian leader who knows the Word. His preaching is carefully constructed, well thought through and usually comprises three points – the holy number for preachers!

Dissatisfaction
Although he maintained a friendship with the Methodist church

of his roots, there was a godly dissatisfaction in Stuart's life as the new church began. He could see the needs of the young people and the fact that traditional church could not meet those needs.

He was also dissatisfied with what he saw in the broader denominational churches. With the re-emphasis on the baptism in the Holy Spirit in the UK, church needed to be more radical. If these young people were to progress in their faith, they needed a model that was closer to the story of Pentecost than to the story of maintaining buildings and traditions.

As Lincoln Free Church began, Stuart was looking beyond Lincoln for help and inspiration. And that help and inspiration was to come from three people in particular: Tony Stone, Jean Darnall and Gerald Coates.

Tony was a fellow Youth for Christ worker. He had his own column in *Buzz Magazine,* the essential reading of the day for rock-and-roll Christians. Tony had taken The Advocates under his wing and encouraged their progress. The friendship spilled over into Stuart's post-band days and Tony became an early mentor for Stuart as the new church became established. In fact, it had been Tony who had first suggested to Stuart back in his days of travelling with the band that there was more to come in terms of a pastoral call for Stuart, and again it was Tony's encouragement that led to the more formal training.

Apostolic Call

Stuart first met Jean Darnall at a meeting in Newark. He had taken a group of newly saved youngsters to an event called Kelham Clinic. This was organised by Vic Ramsey, who had recently opened a work with ex-drug addicts. The young people had not been very well behaved to the extent that Stuart was admonished by one of the leaders who told him that if he couldn't control his young people, they would have to leave.

This had all been observed by Jean, who was speaking that night. She came over to have a quiet word.

'Just to let you know I'd much rather be speaking to your crowd than to these others. I wonder whether I could come and visit you?'

This was quite something. Jean had a well-known preaching and healing ministry in the UK and had been particularly used by God in opening up established churches to the work of the Holy Spirit in what was becoming known as the Charismatic Renewal. She and her husband were from the States but settled in England and worked for many years with different organisations, speaking on the baptism in the Holy Spirit and on healing.

To have such a well-known woman of God ask to come over for tea was both surprising and exciting.

It was as Jean sat with Stuart and Irene that she explained that she felt God had given her a specific word for them.

'Stuart, you are leading a small group at this time, but I believe God would say to you that you will be leading a large strategic church and that God is calling you as an apostle. You will end up leading a network of churches across the nation.'

Stuart sat there dumbfounded. He couldn't help thinking, 'Has she got the right person? Is she confusing me with someone else?'

For a long time historically in the UK, the role of the apostle had been discounted as something that had died out with the early Apostles in the Bible, but in recent times it has been re-established. The role of the apostle was being taught again in those early days of the house churches. The ministries of Ephesians chapter 4 were once more being highlighted with the idea that such ministries worked together in the church and that just as the pastor and teacher had never died out in the church, nor should the apostle or the prophet.

It was one thing to teach that apostles still existed. It was another thing entirely to be told that you *are* one!

Jean was aware of the changing age around her – she saw that the world needed communicators. Not just traditional evangelists but communicators in the media, on film, in literature, in commerce and finance. She saw the need for a new reflection of Church in the nation, a move away from traditional denominations and staid, formal meetings. In Stuart she saw something of the new.

Jean became a dear friend and travelled many times to teach and preach at Lincoln and at numerous events. On one occasion Jean was used in Stuart's healing. Stuart had been diagnosed with a fast heart rhythm which often kept him awake at night – something which had caused concern during his days in The Advocates. Stuart received plenty of prayer from the band and from other friends, but the breakthrough came when Jean Darnall prayed for healing from the platform of a conference Stuart attended. He was instantly healed and has had no heart issues since.

Jean Darnall had also been involved in a number of nationwide initiatives such as the musicals *Come Together* and *The Witness*, and it was this work that brought further contact with Stuart. The Advocates had worked in Lincoln with some of the *Come Together* choirs and, with a good voice, Stuart had been part of the choir. He also went on to be a soloist in *Miracle,* a musical written by Chris Bowater.

And a postscript to this friendship: in her old age, Stuart visited Jean in Los Angeles. A precious final time together. And a farewell to a lady who encouraged and developed Stuart's ministry, considering him to be a spiritual son.

Team Links

Gerald Coates recognised in Stuart someone that God was using and was going to use beyond the confines of a local church. Having heard of Gerald's growing national ministry, Stuart invited him to an early celebration; the first time they met, and the beginning of a lifelong friendship. In a similar way to Jean Darnall, Gerald saw the weight of ministry on Stuart's shoulders and wanted to help.

The help was very practical. As a pioneer of the house church movement, Gerald was a few years ahead of Stuart in developing a church network. He invited Stuart to join him in London on a monthly basis as he met with his own team and developed what became known as the Pioneer Network. Gerald never asked Stuart to join Pioneer, recognising the greater calling on Stuart, but was keen to help develop Stuart's gifting and thinking.

For Stuart's part, meeting Gerald opened his eyes to the broader working of the Holy Spirit in the UK church at that time. Stuart had been aware of the move of the Holy Spirit, but this had been reflected in special meetings and concerts rather than churches. It was only as Stuart's friendship with Gerald developed that he began to realise that what was happening at Lincoln was happening right through the country.

There is no doubt that many of those early gatherings in Lincoln with other leaders were helped and informed by what Stuart observed in Pioneer, particularly the way that Gerald led his team and handled the leaders' meetings. There remained a close personal friendship between Stuart and Gerald which only ended recently with Gerald's death.

Influence

With the move to Newport Hall, the local church grew rapidly, doubling in number to around 120 adults.

This new type of church was causing interest among other churches both in Lincoln and further afield. Lincoln Free Church was increasingly seen as part of the broader movement in the UK, along with other house churches and churches that were shifting out of denominational structures. The interest was further promoted by ministers attending Bible Weeks, one of the first being the Dales Bible Week at Harrogate. Here, church leaders would be encouraged – but also challenged. Many new churches in the UK find their roots back in decisions taken at Bible Weeks in the 1970s and 80s to move out of denominations and start again.

For Stuart, one of the first invitations to come and help was from a group in Grimsby. Ex-Methodists, they saw in Stuart someone who had travelled the same road but who was ahead of them in the journey. Stuart travelled up to Grimsby for six Wednesdays in a row to speak and encourage. Eventually Dave Kitchen, Stuart's cousin and long-time friend from the band, would move there to help lead.

It was a natural outworking of the link with Grimsby to begin to gather such leaders together on a regular basis. Ground Level was birthed from both friendship and necessity.

Ground Level

'What can church look like?'

Stuart sat in a circle with half a dozen leaders at Newport Hall that first morning. Most were from the Lincoln area, plus the leaders from Grimsby. And his question was why they were there.

This once-a-month meeting began to grow as others heard of it. Mainly men in ministry with some having stepped out into new settings because of the work of the Holy Spirit. They represented church fellowships with believers newly baptised in the Holy Spirit. They had started open meetings on Sundays with prophecy and speaking in tongues. They were introducing new songs, with extensive use of the *Songs of Fellowship* series. As the Holy Spirit moved, fellowships were finding an increased depth of friendship and relationship, well beyond previous experience.

But how to handle all this? How to appoint leaders? What boundaries to set? How to manage finances? So many questions for churches released from denominations but without the structures they were once reliant upon.

As the Tuesday morning meetings at Newport Hall developed and friendships formed, they were given a title: Ground Level. It was Stuart's name, reflecting his belief that things needed to be kept real. As Christians we are seated in heavenly places (Ephesians 2:6) but that needs to be worked out in our day-to-day lives at ground level.

There wasn't really a launch date for Ground Level – it was much more a process, a discussion amongst friends. Considering practical things at ground level.

Stuart remembers the day when pastors came from as far away as Hull and King's Lynn.

'Welcome to everyone, from the Humber to the Wash.'

That was it. The Humber to the Wash. Stuart had stumbled upon part of the early vision for Ground Level. That's what he would be doing – serving churches from the Humber to the Wash. A clear region with clear boundaries along the north-east coast and across Lincolnshire.

Dave Kitchen, working as Stuart's administrator, sent letters out to every Pentecostal and Charismatic church he knew of between the Humber and the Wash, inviting them to respond to the vision to reach this specific area. Around thirty churches responded positively to this.

Stuart had found his calling. Ground Level. Humber to the Wash. And as a facilitator to these churches, not as a leader. He was there to support and encourage, not to form and direct.

The Reluctant Leader

This was a very different mandate from others in the nation at the time. Bryn Jones with the Harvestime fellowships (later called Covenant Ministries) out of the Dales Bible Week had a very clear understanding – you were either part of it or you weren't. Terry Virgo, starting up in the south of England under Bryn's initial direction, also formed a movement, eventually called Newfrontiers, which churches were invited to join. Even Gerald had a process of belonging to Pioneer.

For Stuart, it was never that. It was friends getting together to help each other on the journey. Pastors had no need to leave a particular denomination, but they could still be part of Ground Level.

Nevertheless, there was a gradual endorsement of Stuart's leadership. It was discussed at one of the meetings.

'I hope you don't mind me raising this,' said one of the leaders, 'but I want us to be clear. We're just a group of pastors meeting together. But we're also part of something. Ground Level is a wonderful resource and support. And it has a leader. If it were not for Stuart, all this wouldn't exist. Most of us would never have met. I think we need to be clear, Stuart is the leader of Ground Level.'

The reluctant leader, yes. But clearly leading Ground Level? Yes.

As Ground Level formed, churches came and went. Dave Kitchen remembers an early encouragement from David Pawson. He spoke to the group on accountability and working together. The words were too strong for some, and a number of church leaders left Ground Level at that time. But this proved to be a help rather than a hindrance as those that stayed were the ones willing to embrace working together in a meaningful way.

One of those ways was to be a Bible Week called Grapevine.

By the time of the fourth Grapevine Bible Week in 1985, Stuart is writing in *Grapevine News* with clarity and direction for this new movement of churches:

> Since our last Grapevine, we have experienced a year of exciting happenings in our region – a growing unity and clarity of vision, development and release of ministries, church growth and planting. It is this sense of being part of what God is doing which gives added expectancy . . . Three years ago, we took a step of faith based on a God-given desire and vision to take our region – from the Humber to the Wash – for Christ. The cloud was no bigger than a man's hand, but it is becoming an abundance of rain . . . What started as a vision is becoming a reality. Something born in the hearts of a group of local ministers a few years ago has progressed to the point where Grapevine threatens to outgrow the Lincolnshire Showground facilities.

If Ground Level has a DNA, surely it is a combination of clarity of purpose linked to a reflective and pastoral approach to the movement. Such a gradual shaping has brought dividends over the years. More strongly led movements have failed as the leader dies or moves on, but the broader and more relational movements have survived.

In those early days, Stuart was viewed as 'woolly' by other national leaders, who had a more formal membership. Neither was he at the cutting edge of what was happening. There was a natural caution not to exaggerate, not to over-stress any particular teaching. Stuart was teased that his approach represented 'the radical middle ground'. He is happy to accept the label. The test of time shows Stuart's wisdom. What friend Pete Atkins calls Stuart's 'consistent, long-term wisdom and advice' has brought about a steady growth. Ground Level continues to this day, gathering around eighty pastors from churches across the UK.

It is friendship and unity formed around vision that has energised Ground Level. The basis of friendship has resulted in a strong movement, an annual leaders' conference and a regular Bible week in the form of Grapevine (later to be called The One Event).

With the hindsight of today, it can be argued that Stuart sits at the 'restoration table' of pioneers. The concept of the restoration of the church in modern times, along with a theology of a triumphant church, comes from people such as Arthur Wallis. A student of revival, Arthur began to gather others around him, including people such as Bryn Jones, Terry Virgo, Barney Coombs, Gerald Coates, John Noble and Roger Forster. Stuart is younger but is very much in that same mould. His success with Ground Level and the influence it has had on the UK Church suggests that he deserves to be listed with these same men.

All of this from someone who accepts he is a reluctant leader. Someone who works best as a friend and a mentor. Someone who must be encouraged by other leaders to speak at events. Someone with an apostolic call on his life but who appears to be surprised by it.

Grapevine

The leaders that Stuart had started to gather had a problem. How to convey all that God was doing and saying back to their respective congregations? Surely they needed to somehow meet together? Clearly there must be room for a bigger gathering, a broader reflection of what God had started to do with the leaders. The answer was Grapevine. With one eye on the Bible Weeks happening over the summer months, a one-day event was arranged at the Lincolnshire Showground, on August Bank Holiday Saturday, 1982.

There had been an earlier Christian meeting on the Showground in the form of Freshground, a joint youth event from Youth for Christ and the YMCA, and this also pointed to the potential success of a Bible Week.

Stuart had booked the event in faith. Dave Kitchen remembers the response of John Shelbourne from Evangel Church.

'Stuart, it's easier to get forgiveness rather than permission. Well done on booking the Showground. We're with you.'

The words from John are prophetic in another way too. John and Stuart were destined to work together in the future.

There were no booking processes at that first Grapevine, people just came. Around 1,750 gathered.

The first speakers at that initial event were Eddie Smith and David Pawson. Stuart had been greatly encouraged with all the David Pawson cassettes he had listened to over the years, particularly when travelling with The Advocates, so he was an obvious choice. And there had been some contact with David locally – one Sunday he had arrived at Lincoln Free Church, sitting at the back. It turned out he was visiting his sister nearby, so called in on that Sunday. David became a real encourager to Stuart in those early days of church.

Restoration

Ground Level had a success on their hands. People flocked to Grapevine and the format grew to an established five days from Friday to Tuesday each August Bank Holiday. Jean Darnall was the main speaker in year two and by 1985 Gerald Coates was a regular. Other notable speakers in the 80s included Terry Virgo speaking on the restoration of the Church and John Noble speaking of revival and renewal in the Church.

The restoration of the Church was a constant theme, reflecting the new church movement and an awakening of understanding of the centrality of the Church to God's kingdom and purposes.

On the one hand, the restoration vision promoted the gathering of churches with an increased purpose and direction. On the other, it also affected the individual – a literal restoration of the soul. Grapevine became an annual celebration of changed lives, salvation, baptisms in water, baptisms in the Spirit, a renewed vision and sense of vocation, physical healing, relationships restored and so much more.

A team was built to oversee the event. This included Stuart, Dave Kitchen and worship leader Chris Bowater. A full children's ministry was developed as well as a youth programme supported by British Youth for Christ. Chris Bowater led the worship, accompanied by guest musicians such as Noel Richards. Over time, Chris increased the number of musicians, with trumpets, trombones and clarinets supporting keyboards, guitar and drums.

Grapevine began to influence the national scene with teaching cassettes being distributed and Chris Bowater's songs becoming essential material for the average church worship group. His declarative 'Jesus Shall Take the Highest Honour' and reflective 'Faithful God' remain among the best and most significant worship songs of a generation.

Chris wanted to reflect in worship the values Stuart was reflecting in the breadth of different speakers and teaching. Chris deliberately brought in different styles of worship over the Grapevine years. Not just musicians from other churches forming a mini orchestra, but well-known worship leaders and lesser-known teams from farther afield such as from Portugal one year and the United States another. All this was superimposed with rehearsal schools before the event and then practices every day for the week before the start.

The orchestra grew as well. By the early 1990s there was an almost full strings section which proved powerful in accompanying some of the slower worship songs, such as 'Thank You for the Cross' and 'When I Survey'.

This Needs Your Voice

Always hesitant to appear to promote himself, Stuart saw his role much the same way as he saw the leading of Ground Level – a facilitator for what God wanted to do. He chose not to speak at those first few Bank Holiday events. That was until a conversation with John Noble.

'Stuart, why are you not speaking on the main stage?'

'Well, we have our speakers, John, I'm not sure I'm needed.'

'Yes, you are! This event needs your voice!'

It was true of course. Without the direction and assured leadership from Stuart, it was in danger of becoming an oasis for the thirsty soul without carrying any longer-term direction or impetus. Gerald Coates added to the call, declaring in the *Grapevine News* that those attending needed to 'listen, respond and absorb all you can. Only such an attitude will save this current activity of the Spirit from ending in an endless sermon-tasting exercise'.

And to ensure that happened, Stuart's apostolic input would be needed. His quiet, reflective style, yet radical words, found its home in the final Sunday talk at each event – what his good friend Pete Atkins calls Stuart's 'State of the Union address'. Aware that the Sunday night talk was attended by many local churches too, Stuart would often speak of unity – unity, not uniformity. Practically, it brought leaders and churches together at different levels and with one purpose.

The talk was a mix of reflection over the past year and a call to arms for all that lay ahead. Stuart weaved clear strategy into his talk and applied it to the churches. There was a perspective, too, on the nation as a whole, and the effect of the Church upon it. Big picture and detailed application together.

The hesitant preacher was becoming the Holy Spirit directed apostle.

CHAPTER SIX
THE FREEDOM AND THE FIRE

There was a friendly shout from the door of the Evangel Assemblies of God Church as Stuart passed by.

'How are you, Pastor Stuart? God bless you!'

And they were gone. The greeter may have gone, but a thought hadn't. Why is it we all pass each other by, wish each other well, but don't work together? The question was as much to himself as a prayer to God. Lincoln Free Church and Evangel had a similar passion for the city. The worship seemed similar. The leadership had been encouraging of Stuart stepping out into ministry and supportive of the first Grapevine. So, why the separation?

'We've Been Praying for You to Come'

Two weeks later and at the end of a busy day, Stuart was celebrating his thirty-second birthday. The meal had been eaten and the cake cut. The kids were either in bed or watching television.

'What is it, Stuart?'

There was a quizzical look on his face; not hard for Irene to identify.

'Hmm. I just feel I should go to Evangel tonight.'

'You need to go then.'

Ever the practical one, as well as being very perceptive to what the Holy Spirit was saying, Irene was ready to sacrifice the rest of the evening.

Evangel Assemblies of God met in an old United Reformed Church building. Near the city centre, it attracted attention. The place was requiring attention and needed considerable maintenance. Still with the organ and pews in situ, the inside was also in need of change.

This was the building that Stuart slipped into that night. The meeting was already underway. Stuart positioned himself behind a pillar way back in the building and began to enjoy the worship. The church was led by John Shelbourne, assisted by an excellent Bible teacher, John Phillips. It was John Shelbourne leading that night, and if Stuart had hoped to stay hidden, it didn't last long.

'Brother Stuart is here tonight. Come to the front, brother – share your heart with us.'

So there it was. That first time together.

Stuart spoke on what was on his heart and the reason for being there that night. How sad it was that as churches in the city, they never worked together. They had the same vision and the same passion for the lost, but continued to work on their own, rather than together.

'It's sad that we pass each other by on the street when we believe the same. Rather than pass each other by, let's try and walk together.'

Stuart finished and sat down as the church shared and prayed some more.

It was an excited John Shelbourne and John Phillips who approached Stuart at the end of the meeting.

'We've been praying for you to come. We had a prophecy a few weeks ago about working together. And here you are! We need to continue to talk!'

And so they did.

First Conversations

First conversations were promising. John and John were not typical Assemblies of God pastors and had been significantly influenced by the house church movement, particularly by Bryn Jones and the Dales Bible Week.

It meant that the three leaders were able to agree on a lot. What began as a working together of two churches picked up pace in the discussions. A merger of the two churches. A new start. A new name. And a move by John and John away from the Assemblies of God denomination. This last one proved to be particularly tricky.

It wasn't long before both the Lincoln Free Church and Evangel Church names had been dropped. The 120 members of Lincoln Free Church and the 300 or so at Evangel were together on a new journey. Welcome to the world, New Life Christian Fellowship Lincoln.

Changes at first were gradual and well managed. The three leaders were aiming for the best from both churches. Stuart's relaxed style, John Shelbourne's preaching, John Phillips' Bible teaching. Each found their place within the new church. Sunday mornings were together. Sunday evenings were separate so that Stuart and Irene could continue to lead some of the original congregation and help them adjust to the new. It was the best of both worlds.

Friendships grew. Leaders learned to work together. There was a freedom across the church. An awareness that the new name reflected a new life in the believers.

Differences

As time went on, some of the boundaries between the old and new began to blur. But not all of them. And as the joining of the churches became more complete, differences between Stuart and the two Johns also became more apparent.

Maybe it had been a bit naïve to think that because God was on the case, the merger would go through without any problems. The more formal style of Evangel was still on show and this presented a problem to Stuart. Irene was concerned, too, having always had a more measured view of the initiative.

John and John still wore ties. They still came over to Stuart's house clasping a Bible in hand, even when it was for a social event. The structure of the meetings was still more formal than Stuart was used to. The Pentecostal 'thus says the Lord' prophecies were unhelpful. Bearing in mind Stuart and Irene had left the formality of the Methodists some years earlier, there was no wish to go back to that kind of meeting structure. The freedoms that the newly emerging church began to enjoy were being pushed back by the strength of Pentecostal tradition within the larger unit, the original Evangel congregation.

At the meetings themselves, the worship team was almost entirely from the Evangel side. Chris Bowater, leading the worship, already had a UK-wide presence. His musicals had travelled the country and his style was imprinted onto the local church worship at New Life. The main leaders of the welcome team, the set-up team and most of the children's work were also from an Evangel background. In the Sunday morning meeting, the church elders still sat on the stage facing the congregation.

Perhaps the most obvious pointer to all not being well was the way the congregation from the Evangel side addressed the three leaders: 'Pastor John, Mr Phillips and Stuart'. It had never been the intention of the two Johns for Stuart to be the junior partner, but that was how it was looking.

In the formal discussion documents of Evangel before the merger, there are some loose words that suggest Lincoln Free Church was being taken over. It does not appear to have been intentional, but the words suggest that it wasn't quite as clear as it should have been.

Phrases used by all three leaders during early discussions such as 'I'll die if you do' seemed to have been taken differently by each party. Evangel was finding it hard to die. Lincoln Free Church had died but its former members were wondering what exactly had been raised to life. And behind it all was the Assemblies of God denomination.

The new church hadn't quite left the Assemblies of God. Stuart and Irene had no wish to have left one denomination with the Methodists only to join another with the Assemblies of God.

It was tricky. John Phillips was on the AOG executive. Both Johns had been part of Assemblies of God for many years. But surely, for the sake of unity and vision . . .

Elders' meetings at that time were lengthy affairs. It seemed to Stuart that things were agreed with elders but then promptly forgotten and not enacted.

Input from others was irregular but consistent in theme. Gerald Coates threw in the odd hand grenade with his hatred for anything that looked religious rather than Christlike. Bryn Jones was counselling clear authority and order among the leaders. Even David Pawson, someone from an entirely different background, was saying to Stuart, 'Either stay in there and be bold or just get out!'

A prophecy from Jonny Barr, an itinerant teacher, was helpful. He saw the church as a glider, but still attached to the aeroplane. There was a need to cut the rope. Stuart saw this as relating to the Assemblies of God link. John and John weren't so sure.

In the end, the two Johns agreed to leave the Assemblies of God. This was certainly a help, but tensions persisted.

Six Years

The tensions lasted six years.

Six years of internal tensions, the right words and the wrong actions. Six years of help and advice but with limited follow through. Stuart would travel with John Shelbourne to meetings and John would be very clear in their discussions. But back in Lincoln again, change was complex.

It was easier for Stuart. Of course it was. He had left the Methodists a long time ago. For John and John, there was a considerable amount of tradition still to deal with. But it had to be dealt with. Change was needed.

All this came to a head in a meeting with Bryn Jones. All three men felt he could provide the help needed. Bryn, leader of Covenant Ministries and founder of the Dales Bible Week, was known to all three and hence was seen as someone who would be unencumbered by friendship or history with one or the other.

Bryn asked each to share what they felt was the correct next step. When Stuart's turn came, he cleared his throat. Shifting uncomfortably and aware of what he was about to say, Stuart started by commending the two Johns for their leadership.

'But, Bryn, we have landed in a kind of middle ground that is neither one thing nor the other. We need to be more intentional about change. The only way I can see for us to get out of this uncertainty still intact as a church is to ask all the elders to stand down and to start again. There are too many voices, too much confusion. We need a much smaller leadership body of five or six people, including the three of us. The whole thing is too unwieldy and the past links to the Assemblies of God still affect us.'

Conversations continued. Bryn indicated it was time to finish the meeting and, with that, set out what he thought was best.

'Stuart has seen it clearly. That's what you need to do.'

It was with some relief that both Johns agreed with Bryn. But the moment the three were back in the car, the tone of the conversation changed. It was very evident that the two Johns were going to find this difficult.

'But we have to do it!' Stuart was adamant. 'If you want me to, I will go round on Friday and see all the elders personally, asking each of them to step down.'

Both Johns agreed.

That Friday turned out to be a long day.

Round the Houses

Stuart felt strongly that after six years of going round the houses with regard to the big issues, it was time to move on.

And that's what he said to each of the elders that day as he, accompanied by another elder, literally went around the houses.

Stuart went over to his dad's first. Then to a lovely gentleman called David Wright. Both saw the issues and agreed to stand down with a grace and with an excitement for the next chapter.

It got harder as the day went on, until finally there was one elder left to visit. It was nearly midnight by this time and Stuart had been telephoning ahead each time to keep to some kind of schedule.

As he approached the door, it was opened.

'Stop there! I know why you've come. I am not going to give you the opportunity of standing me down. I resign!'

And with that, the door was shut.

And the job was done.

New Freedom

Some changes were immediate and obvious. Others were changed step by step. Gone was the overly formal structure. Gone (thankfully) were the everlasting elders meetings.

Stuart had a new freedom in his leadership. And so did the two Johns, which they began to appreciate. In fact, John Shelbourne was genuinely excited at the possibilities of travelling with a more evangelistic ministry. John Phillips continued with Bible teaching, something that brought genuine support to Stuart.

Over a period of time, some of the elders were reappointed, among them Stuart's dad and David Wright.

The meetings were free. The church grew. All was well.

Reflecting on that time, Chris Bowater believes John Shelbourne had some kind of premonition of passing the baton to Stuart as the church changed. One night Chris went into the building to play and practise on the keyboard. John Shelbourne was already there – at the front of the church, on his hands and knees, crying out to God.

It was to be the last time Chris saw John alive.

Death

Stuart was over at a prayer day at the National Exhibition Centre in Birmingham. He was on the platform, helping to lead the day with thousands together praying for the nation.

But it was hard to concentrate. Something was wrong. Stuart had a real feeling of disquiet.

This was 1988. Well before the days of mobile phones, so it was not easy to call home. Stuart was aware that their son Andrew had not been well and he was concerned that the disquiet was to do with that.

On arriving home, he learned that Andrew had been rushed to hospital earlier that day and had had an emergency operation to remove his appendix. All had gone well and Irene had taken the decision not to try and contact Stuart.

It was with some relief that Stuart went to bed that night, sure that his anxiety during the day had been to do with Andrew.

The phone rang at around 11.30pm. It was Rosie, daughter-in-law to John Shelbourne.

'Stuart, you need to get to the hospital. John is dying.'

Picking up Chris Bowater on the way, Stuart and Chris arrived at the hospital to learn that they were too late.

A heart attack, aged fifty-five.

It was hard to know what to do. Stuart and Chris did their best to comfort and pray with the family. Muriel, John's wife, was there of course. They prayed with her, held her, cried with her. They had to get a message to John's youngest son, who was away on a Christian camp.

It was a long night.

Responsibility

Stuart may be a reluctant leader, but he can most certainly lead. And this is what he did now.

There needed to be clarity, assurance, certainty as to the way forward.

John Phillips was sure that Stuart should become the main leader. He promised to stay and support.

In fact, John remained part of the church until his own death at the age of ninety-six. He continued to teach and continued to support Stuart. He had started preaching as a young boy and was still teaching from the Bible in his nineties. Possibly his greatest ministry was in Brazil, where he was considered an apostle, reaching hundreds of thousands with the gospel and planting hundreds of churches. John served churches in the most inhospitable parts of that nation, often travelling by boat through the Amazon tributaries.

John Phillips' profound understanding of Scripture was a great help to Stuart. Often, when there was controversy, John would go back to the Word, dig deep and prepare a positional paper for leadership review. John was greatly affected in the 1990s Holy Spirit awakening in the UK and his ministry blossomed all over again as a result.

John Shelbourne's death was addressed directly. The congregation were assured that the church would continue to move forward and would retain all the good things that John had brought to it.

Stuart began to preach most Sundays, setting out a vision for New Life Christian Fellowship.

At the same time, he was helping the family and those closest to John. The funeral was at New Life, with a later thanksgiving service at the cathedral.

A few people left the church, saying that they had lost their pastor.

But there was a pastor. Stuart stepped up.

Incremental Change

After such a devastating event, it was best to be careful; to make change, but at a pace that would be appreciated rather than resented. John Phillips continued to preach and to publicly endorse Stuart as the new senior pastor, ably supported by Paul Dando, who had moved from Wales to join the team. Chris Bowater continued to lead the worship. The team leaders stayed in place.

But little by little, things began to change. Some of the more traditional elements of church life were set aside. The white cloth for communion. The more formal dress for Sunday meetings. The hushed tones before a meeting began . . .

Gerald Coates was extremely helpful in this. With antennae for anything 'religious', he was able to not only identify what needed to change, but to bring some of the teaching as well. Gerald was generous with his time, helping Stuart and Irene become established as the senior leaders.

Others reached out to help as well, notably Terry Virgo from Newfrontiers. Other Ground Level leaders were quick to get alongside and pray. Stuart was not on his own in this journey.

And it was well that he was not alone. The stress did show. Irene went into premature labour. Stuart got shingles.

Some within Assemblies of God were not as helpful as others and added to the pressure Stuart was feeling. In fact, one publication suggested that John Shelbourne had died of a broken heart, questioning Stuart's over-influence with the coming together of the churches.

This was not the general view from within the church though, and prayer support continued from the church and from other friends, other pastors, other streams.

The church began to grow; to blossom in fact. Stuart's persistence for change, but delivered with such grace and care, meant that most, even those closest to John Shelbourne, stayed with the church. It helped that John Phillips was still very active. Muriel, John Shelbourne's widow, helped too. As she came through a time of grief, she came into a time of ministry. She was an able preacher, so to have her speaking on a Sunday with such commitment to the church under Stuart's leadership was a blessing to both her and the church as a whole.

Change in the church practices and growth in the church were hand in hand. Stuart's good friend Jeff Lucas notes that when traditional sacred cows needed to be slaughtered, Stuart was not afraid to do so. But his gentle manner meant that when change came, it was managed with wisdom and care. In other words, you may not have noticed that the sacred cow was slaughtered until it ceased breathing!

Stuart was finding his feet, both within New Life Lincoln and beyond. His gentle but assured approach to ministry was attracting interest. His list of invitations to teach and preach was growing. As the decade changed and the 1990s began, Stuart was increasingly seen as an apostle, establishing and growing churches. His teaching, always gracious, was also challenging. His awareness of the need for change within the UK church was reflected in his preaching. He was invited by many across a range of churches both in the UK and around the world. A man who spoke radically but in such a gentle manner.

The reluctant leader was turning into the non-threatening radical.

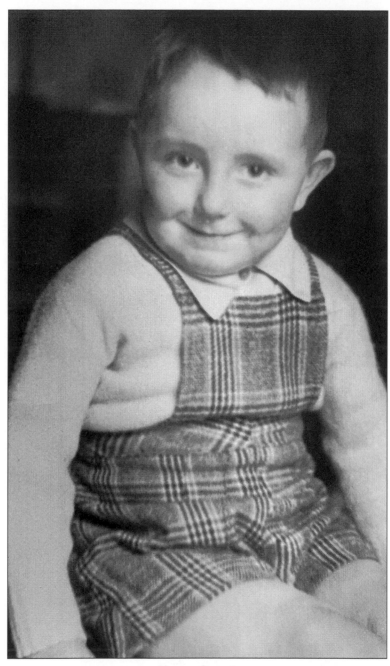

Young Stuart

The Bell Family – Stuart shows off music festival awards

Graham, Elizabeth and Stuart

Future football captain

Stuart Bell and The Advocates

The Advocates Rehearsal Time

The Advocates at Lincoln Castle

Stuart takes vocal lead

Team and speakers at Grapevine Celebration

John Phillips at Grapevine 1985

Stuart and John Shelbourne, Grapevine 1985

Ground Level Team with guest speakers Terry Virgo
and Tony Morton

New Life wider leadership team

Big Top crowd at Grapevine Celebration

One Event crowd with Bishop Tony Miller

Andrew receiving National Primary School Teacher of the Year
Award 2007

Becki and Glen's wedding day

Dave and Sarah's wedding day

Stuart and Irene with Gerald and Anona Coates

Stuart and Irene with Jack and Trish Groblewski

Stuart receiving his British Empire Medal 2015

Outside Number 10 after a national church leaders' gathering
with Theresa May

Irene – wife of 50 years

CHAPTER SEVEN
THE SPIRIT AND THE SERVANT

'This is so exciting, Stuart! Something is happening. The Holy Spirit is doing something new in our churches.'

Gerald was on the phone.

He'd just spent time with John and Ellie Mumford, leaders of the Vineyard churches in the UK. Ellie had herself recently returned from a church called Toronto Airport Vineyard in Canada. Led by Pastors John and Carol Arnott, they had invited a guest to speak: Randy Clark. As Randy shared on how God had miraculously healed him after a car accident, the Holy Spirit began to move.

The anointing Randy carried was seeing an outworking in the meetings at Toronto. The impact was such that Randy was asked to stay on. The meetings grew in number and the work of the Holy Spirit grew in power. Many at the meetings were overcome by the Spirit, finding themselves on the floor as people prayed for them. There was a lot of laughter – waves of laughter through the auditorium – and a lot of noise.

There was a real awareness of the Holy Spirit's presence. It brought about a holiness, a desire to be free from sin and anything that held people back from pursuing God.

Ellie had carried this blessing back to the UK. And now others, Gerald among them, were also benefiting from this new move of the Holy Spirit.

RT Kendall

One of those at a meeting with Ellie Mumford was the well-known Bible teacher RT Kendall. At the time he was still the pastor of Westminster Chapel, a noted evangelical church with an international impact.

RT arrived for a midweek meeting at New Life in Lincoln off the back of his meeting with Ellie and a number of other leaders at Holy Trinity Church, Brompton. But he was a bit unsure as to what had happened. Initially, he had been wary of what he had been hearing from Toronto and was hesitant at first as to whether this was of God.

Before the midweek meeting, Stuart took RT for a meal. RT explained his position and described what had happened at Holy Trinity Brompton. Ellie and a number of leaders had prayed for RT but he had felt nothing.

'Well, Dr Kendall, you really shouldn't just rely on your feelings, you know. Perhaps you are a carrier of the blessing.'

The words were out of Stuart's mouth before he had time to consider the wisdom of them. Here was one of the primary Bible scholars of recent times, serving as the pastor of the very same church previously led by the great Dr Martyn Lloyd-Jones, and here was a pastor from Lincoln challenging him on his feelings!

RT became quiet. There was a frown on his face. Oh dear. Stuart really had done it this time. He'd managed to upset one of his heroes of the faith in just one sentence!

'Yes,' said RT, 'I'd like to know whether I am a carrier of the blessing.'

Despite RT announcing that he was unaffected by what had happened in the meeting with Ellie Mumford, Stuart couldn't help noticing that RT was laughing a lot throughout the meal. In fact, the laughter was so loud at times, it was fetching glances from people at other tables. Stuart said nothing.

Later that evening, after the church meeting had finished, RT was in Stuart's office along with Chris Bowater and one or two others.

'Maybe I should pray for you,' said RT, 'in case I *am* carrying this blessing. And if anything does happen, please do write and let me know.'

The next day, Stuart begins to share some of the Toronto story with another leader. The impact is immediate. The leader starts to laugh uncontrollably.

An hour later and a meeting with two of his own leaders, again Stuart witnesses the Holy Spirit come. One is shaking uncontrollably. The other is flat out on the floor.

This has not happened to Stuart before. Something had happened to him. Last night.

A letter went off to RT the same day, explaining what had happened after his visit and suggesting that he indeed was a carrier of this blessing even if he felt nothing himself. A note came back a couple of days later from RT. It simply said, 'WOW!'

Come and See

The very next day Stuart called a meeting for the whole church. Stuart shared what had happened with RT and the story of the

Toronto church. Immediately the Holy Spirit moved in power. The building was packed with people eager to hear about the Toronto Blessing. Many of them received the blessing that night.

There was an excitement in the church. Pretty much everyone was affected. Mature and perhaps what might be called more conservative members of the congregation were seen rolling around the floor in fits of laughter. Members of the congregation who, for years, had been struggling with repetitive sin, were set free. There was healing. There was laughter. There was freedom. People were full of the Holy Spirit. Shaking, laughter, roaring in the Spirit, a sense of fire in the bones, a burning in the hands, a rise of faith for healing . . . all these phenomena became part of each and every meeting at New Life.

Stuart sent out an invitation to other leaders, explaining what had happened since RT's visit and inviting them to come along.

Meetings, called 'Refreshing Meetings', became daily affairs, unstructured for the most part, with everyone enjoying God's obvious presence with them. The fire was caught. Many churches within Ground Level and farther afield were catching the same blessing and taking it back with them. The Toronto Blessing was becoming a UK Blessing.

Around this time, Stuart was invited to speak at an Ichthus conference – the group of churches led by Roger Forster. It was clear to Stuart at the end of his talk that the spiritual climate in the room was rising. Roger asked Stuart to pray for him. About halfway through the prayer, Stuart was taken totally by surprise as he and Roger were knocked to the floor by the Holy Spirit, staying there for about twenty minutes. Stuart felt the power and love of God like 'warm waves' passing over him.

As the conference continued, there were manifestations of laughter, tears, confession of sin, humility and brokenness. For over five hours, as the meeting continued, there was a very evident blessing of God upon those attending.

The Holy Spirit was at work with Irene as well during this time. Usually, Irene would do pretty much anything to keep out of the spotlight. If she were asked to speak, there would be lengthy times of anxious preparation for even the smallest of contributions. Even being asked to say grace for a meal would cause nervousness. But when God began to move through the Toronto Blessing and as Irene received that blessing, things changed.

She noticed it on one day in particular. She and Stuart were in a leaders' meeting arranged by Gerald Coates. At the end of the session, Gerald announced that lunch was ready and asked Irene to say grace. She did so immediately, with confidence and without fear. That was the moment she realised that God had been ministering to her in such a way that she had received a new confidence in Him.

Learning More

Stuart was keen to learn and to experience more.

He got into his car and drove down to visit Gerald at one of the Pioneer leaders' meetings. This was at Fairmile Court in Surrey, and the day had been split into a number of sessions.

Actually, the first session became the second session, became the third session . . . the meeting never ended. There were leaders all over the floor, some crying out, some still, all under the power of the Holy Spirit's work. Amusingly, Queen Anne of Romania was expected to arrive for the afternoon session. A committed

Christian and personal friend of Gerald and Anona Coates, Gerald was keen to welcome her.

The problem was, there were bodies all over the floor. There were bodies across the entrance to the room, including Stuart's. Eventually Gerald had to climb out of the window and run to the front of the building to greet Queen Anne.

For Stuart, the time was precious. Away from his daily pastoral responsibilities, he was able to relax. And as he did so, the Holy Spirit ministered to him. It reminded him of the time he was baptised in the Spirit when Arthur Mann had prayed. But there was something more here. It was even more supernatural. The sense of the presence of the Holy Spirit was so powerful, it was a real effort to get up off the floor.

Stuart continued to pursue what was happening. Along with American friend Jack Groblewski, he travelled to Toronto early on in the blessing, keen to receive whatever God had for him through the Holy Spirit.

It would be fair to say that the Toronto Blessing was a watershed moment for Stuart. He would not be the same again. The passion that was always there was stirred even more. The ministry that had developed over the years was set alight again. Faith increased. Miracles increased. Lives were changed. Churches were never the same.

Dealing with the Mess

Any study of revival will highlight a considerable amount of revival 'mess'. This is reflective of lives being changed. Bodies on the floor. People crying out to God. Shaking. Drunkenness in the Spirit. Convulsions. Jumping around. Roaring like a lion. And all of it interrupting the regular form of church meetings.

For some, these interruptions were too wild and too messy for it to be of God. They spoke against the Toronto Blessing.

With a good deal of wisdom, Stuart was able to speak into this. He identified, for example, that a number of church leaders had a problem with people roaring. Using Amos as a source scripture, Stuart taught on God roaring like a lion (Amos 1:2, 3:8). The reflections from Amos were along the lines of 'how can I not respond to God?'

Stuart spoke of a time when two young men leaned over Stuart, who was on the floor at the time, and roared out like lions. Later he observed them crying out in prayer for the poor. Equating the two, Stuart taught that roaring could indeed be Holy Spirit led, often a reflection of what Paul writes in Romans chapter 8:

> We do not know what to pray for as we ought, but the Spirit himself intercedes for us with groanings too deep for words.

In his unassuming way, Stuart was hitting at the heart of many of the criticisms of revival 'mess'. In words that appeared gentle yet carried an authority and a call to repentance, he was pointing out to the critics that caution was needed before saying something was not of God – especially when the Bible speaks of such manifestations.

Invitations

Lincoln became one of the 'hot spots' for the Toronto Blessing in the UK. As a result, Stuart was becoming known beyond his own group of churches and invitations began to arrive from far and wide for him to speak.

Wherever he went he told the same story. RT. Ellie. Toronto.

And the results were the same. Laughter. Falling to the floor.

Rolling around. Increased faith. Healing. A new filling of the Holy Spirit.

Throughout the rest of 1994 and for pretty much all of 1995, Stuart was travelling, teaching and bringing the Holy Spirit gifts and anointing to the churches. He would often describe it as a season of refreshing as set out in Acts chapter 3. Peter is speaking to the crowds. As he speaks first of salvation, he goes on to say that God will bring times of refreshing (verse 19).

'And this is what you are experiencing tonight. Even as I speak, many of you are sensing an increased presence of the Holy Spirit. I am going to invite the Spirit to come in power. All you have to do is be ready to receive . . .'

And from that simple faith statement, Stuart would pray, invite the Holy Spirit and watch Him move. He would have already trained a team – some local, some travelling with Stuart – to minister in much the same way as he had observed in meetings he had been in earlier, in turn copied from Toronto.

People would be lined up at the front of the meeting room with space in between. There would be pray-ers and catchers. And the Holy Spirit would move.

Churches were impacted. The Ground Level movement was impacted. Grapevine was impacted.

Further afield too. Stuart spoke at churches in the United States and closer to home, in France. The French connection was an interesting one. They got hold of a cassette tape of Chris Bowater's music. In their own words, 'We heard on that tape what we heard in the Spirit.' As a result, they travelled to Lincoln and a relationship was formed.

Everywhere the same. Powerful workings of the Holy Spirit. Long meetings. Late nights. Lives transformed.

Even though the nights were long, it was a genuine refreshing. Families were not naturally tired. Children who attended the late-night meetings were able to go to school totally unaffected. Dave Bell remembers it as an absolute treat. To be part of the Holy Spirit awakening even at a young age – and to be allowed to stay up was special too!

In Lincoln, Stuart wanted to be sure that this blessing was not just kept in the church. Evangelist Eric Delve was fascinated with what he was seeing with the Toronto Blessing and volunteered to come up to Lincoln every Friday night, even though he lived in the south of England. These Friday night meetings became the ones to invite visitors to. The ministry would be the same but at some stage in the evening Eric would preach for a short while and many found a new faith in Christ.

The depth of worship the church was experiencing was another reflection of this particular blessing. Chris Bowater found himself in the most fruitful time in his music ministry. As he describes it, 'songs were coming down from heaven and I was catching them'. A good number of Christian worship songs from the Toronto years have remained a part of worship in today's Church.

The blessing was spilling out of the church building in other ways too. People were so drunk in the Spirit that as they left the building they were crawling on all fours, unable to stand. Not long afterwards, the owner of a local pub came to the church and said, 'I had to see what was going on. There's more happening here than in my pub!'

Initially Stuart had been concerned that the outward effects of the blessing would put people off should they not have a Christian faith. He needn't have worried.

Andrew, Stuart and Irene's oldest son, was by now training as a teacher. He invited one of his university colleagues to the meeting. Andrew was a bit concerned as to how she would react to seeing people rolling around the floor laughing and to some of the other phenomena. But he wanted her to be there to hear the gospel message from Eric Delve.

At the end of the evening, Andrew tentatively asked what she had thought.

'I really enjoyed it. It was so normal.'

'What do you mean?' asked Andrew.

'Well, the whole evening seemed really normal. Usually, church is weird with all that standing up and sitting down, singing hymns and the like. This was much more normal!'

The Pittsburgh Blessing

An invitation came in for Stuart to travel to Pittsburgh in Pennsylvania. The inviting church, Church of the Risen Savior, was fairly small by US standards; a congregation of around a hundred people. But when Stuart arrived, the pastors, Bill and Melinda Fish, asked him if he wouldn't mind speaking to a city-wide gathering with a number of churches.

'You see, something's been happening. We got a call from some fellow pastors in the city. There was a prophetic minister in Pittsburgh a few weeks back from South Africa, and he told the churches to be ready, because the Pittsburgh Blessing was on the way. We think you may be the catalyst to that blessing.'

The church leaders were well aware of what had been happening in Toronto and had learned that Stuart had been part of that blessing back in the UK. Hence, it wasn't much of a leap for them to assume that Stuart was the answer to the prophetic word.

It may not have been much of a leap for them, but it was for Stuart!

No Pressure

The corporate gathering was organised by Bishop Joseph Garlington, a well-known minister in his own right. The first service took place in the Greater Works Center and the city was expectant as to what God was going to do.

No pressure then, Stuart.

The building was packed. Churches from across the city had heard of the event and their members were there in numbers. Small churches and megachurches. Methodists and Baptists. Messianic Jews and Episcopalians. Denominational churches and new churches. Blacks, whites, Latinos . . . every race and nation seemed to be there.

Stuart sat on the front row and, as the worship began, looked behind him. There was not a single empty seat.

'Oh Lord, I need your help tonight!'

The worship was God-glorifying. The band were exceptional.

No pressure.

Bishop Joseph introduced Stuart as someone who had been greatly used in the Toronto Blessing. No pressure again.

'Thank you for your warm welcome. I have to say I'm just an ordinary person, a pastor from England. But I have seen God moving greatly in recent times. Let me tell you a story. I have a friend called RT . . .'

Weaving stories of blessing into the Acts 3 preaching of Peter and the times of refreshing promised from the Lord, Stuart took the congregation on a faith journey.

He only spoke for half an hour or so, and at the end of his message Stuart invited all those who would like to receive a blessing prayer to stay behind.

Nobody moved.

Godly Mayhem

With a bit of organisation, half of the congregation went to the gym next door and the other half remained. In both locations, people were lined up in prayer lines with space in between. Pastors and leaders were asked to go along the lines and pray a simple prayer, asking the Holy Spirit to come. Volunteers stood behind each person as 'catchers'. Stuart went between the two venues, praying and declaring the presence of the Spirit in and on each person.

What happened is best described as godly mayhem. People fell to the floor, many of them laughing, many rolling around on the floor. Some shouting out. Others crying. There was such a presence of God in the room it was hard to stay upright.

Many godly people met with their God in a new and intimate way that evening. There was a refreshing, an anointing. People got up off the floor differently from the way they went down – those that could get up that is. A good number had to be carried out of the building and across the car park, still drunk in the Spirit.

Such were the numbers of people, the ministry went on until the early hours of the morning.

'You Can't Go Home'

It was after a late breakfast the next day that a call came through to Bill and Melinda's house. It was Pastor Joseph wanting to speak to Stuart.

'I have no doubt whatsoever that God began a promised move of His blessing last night. I know you are due to go back to the UK in a couple of days, but you have to stay. You can't go back home!'

Bishop Joseph was concerned that what had started needed to continue. There was a need to 'keep the flow' of what the Holy Spirit was doing and not to inhibit Him in any way. That meant nightly meetings. It meant the catalyst needed to stay in town.

Phone calls to Irene. Flight tickets changed.

There began a wonderful work of God. Every night the venues across the city were full. Every night Stuart preached and invited the Holy Spirit to come. Every night the Holy Spirit came. Laughter, shakings, shouting, crying. Every night God's refreshing presence on His people. Churches of all denominations and backgrounds affected. North, south, east and west. Pastors reconciled. Churches working together in new ways.

The meetings went on right through December 1994, breaking for Christmas. That was Stuart's opportunity to go home, but he was back in January, this time with Irene. In fact, theirs was the only flight to get into Pittsburgh airport that day due to heavy snow.

Heavy snow and a heavy Holy Spirit presence. Stuart was at ease with his new mandate. This was God's initiative, and he was honoured to be part of it.

Special leadership gatherings were organised at which Stuart taught. Up to fifty leaders met regularly in Covenant Church, the church led by Bishop Joseph. Stuart spent time ministering to the pastors, encouraging friendship and cooperation across the churches. There was much repentance for attitudes towards each other, many pastors in tears as they expressed their love for each other. Some went further, publicly repenting of wrong attitudes at the evening meetings.

One long-term result of the Pittsburgh Blessing was a city-wide prayer meeting which continued each week for over ten years.

Black Shoes White

A key point of learning for Stuart during his time in Pittsburgh was to ask questions, to go beneath what appeared to be happening on the surface.

On one occasion, a black lady was on the floor sobbing, crying loudly. And then there was a change. She began to laugh and continued laughing wildly for quite some time. At the end of the meeting, Stuart was keen to learn what had been going on.

'Well, pastor, it was as if God took me back to my childhood. We had such a poor upbringing and God was ministering into that, into some of the hurts from childhood, the shame I felt for being so poor. One of the most embarrassing moments for me as a child was my first communion. I'm from a Catholic background and at your first communion, you needed a white dress and white shoes. But we were so poor as a family, we could only afford one pair of shoes, and these were black. I had to go to that communion wearing black shoes.

'As I was on the floor just now, weeping, I saw Jesus come to me. He was wearing a white gown. And then he smiled at me. Lifting His garment slightly, He let me see that He was wearing black shoes!'

Back in the UK and Stuart had been invited to lead the late-night Holy Spirit gathering at the Spring Harvest event in Skegness.

At the back of the meeting stood a black lady. She was from a Catholic background and wasn't sure she should go to this particular gathering. But she stepped inside and found a seat.

She asked God for some sort of sign that she should be there. She said to God, 'Please, let the man at the front say something so that I know I am meant to be here.'

As Stuart began to speak, he told of a black lady in Pittsburgh who had been doubled up crying and then began to laugh. The lady at Spring Harvest leaned forward in her chair.

'He's going to talk about the shoes! He's talking about the shoes!'

As Stuart began to describe the picture of Jesus wearing black shoes, the lady began to cry and laugh at the same time.

She had asked God to confirm she should be there.

In her own childhood, the family were poor. She, too, only had a black pair of shoes for her first communion. The exact thing had happened to her. In her case, her mother had painted the black shoes white for her communion service.

Oceans apart. Different families in different times. But the same story. And a God who loves his daughter enough to answer her prayer that night. Needless to say, not only did that lady stay in the meeting but God deeply ministered to her.

Her final comment as she told the story to Stuart after the meeting: 'This has been the most fantastic evening of my life.'

Toronto Fruit

In addition to Pittsburgh and all that happened in the UK, Stuart was privileged to speak at the Toronto church on five occasions during this time.

One of the most beautiful fruits of the Toronto Blessing during 1994 and 1995 was the way God's people were ministered to at such a deep level. Hurts and scars from earlier years were gently healed by the Holy Spirit. His people found a new energy in their faith, a strength of belief, much of it coming from those quiet moments of the Spirit's ministry as much as from the louder times of laughter and shaking.

Reflecting back, Stuart was thrilled with all that happened. He saw it as a move of the Holy Spirit to support and extend the church in its worship and witness, not a be all and end all of itself. A number of churches changed to 'revival centres' during that time, ditching regular meetings, ending sermons, expecting that the Spirit would speak instead. Perhaps this was unwise as when the season came to an end, they were left with an empty ministry, trying to replicate what the Spirit had been doing – but sadly in their own strength.

The Toronto Blessing was indeed a blessing. But as Stuart was always careful to point out in the various meetings he led during this time, this was not new. There were similar stories throughout church history and Stuart would often tell of them in the meetings – the shakings of the Wesley and Whitefield revivals in the 1700s. The falling to the floor and overflow of tongues at Azusa Street and in the 1904 Welsh Revival.

By putting the Toronto Blessing in the context of history, the work of the Spirit could be appreciated as something that was ongoing, so that as and when the current season ended, there was not the disappointment that affected some churches, but an awareness that the Spirit was simply bringing a different emphasis at a different time.

For Stuart, it was a season that refreshed the Church but it was never intended to change the direction or remit of the Church. The Church in the community continued to have the same call and same reach. The same Great Commission mandate. The New Testament model of Church continued to be the model that should be followed. There was disappointment, of course, that the Toronto Blessing didn't flow into full revival in the nations, but at the same time, churches that stewarded the move well, benefitted and grew.

What a privilege to have served in that way, and on such a large scale, throughout the time of the Toronto Blessing. Especially in Pittsburgh, a moment in time where Stuart received an exceptional calling affecting a city and a region in a way that permanently changed it. An ease of ministry that, looking back, was unusual. A sense of being able to listen to the slightest whispers of the Spirit. A confidence in God that He was there and that He would move.

Chapter Eight
Living In The Good

Did the Toronto Blessing fade or was it a specific period of time from the Lord? Maybe both. Theologians can battle that one out. In the meantime, Stuart and Irene continued to live in the good of all that God did in that time, both in terms of family and personal life and in terms of church. Such an extensive period of being tutored by the Holy Spirit led to further ministry around the world. And at home base, the Lincoln church continued to grow as well.

In fact, the Toronto Blessing had given New Life Christian Fellowship Lincoln an increased faith that God was on the move, and a new measure of anticipation that He could move through each of them.

One of Stuart's constant themes in preaching at this time was of refreshing leading on to purpose:

God isn't interested in just refreshing the Church for some good times. He has sent His refreshing for a divine purpose.

And as the refreshing became a point in modern Church history, the divine purposes of God were still in front of the Church. God had prepared His people for purpose.

'I Am Who I Am'

During the times of refreshing, there was a special moment just for Irene. Growing up, Irene heard stories from her mum of her own upbringing. Mum was left-handed but at the time she was growing up this was frowned upon. Irene's mum was forced to tie her left hand behind her back at school in order to ensure that she would become right-handed.

The picture came back forcibly to Irene, who is also left-handed, during a refreshing meeting. What was God trying to say? Irene became aware that God had no intention of tying a hand behind Irene's back. She was to express herself in the terms that God desired, not how man desired. She was to be who God had made her to be, not what others wanted her to be.

Irene had already been learning during this time that God wanted her to be less fearful and, as a leader and a wife to an apostle, this was a releasing word. Irene took the opportunity to deliberately release the picture she was seeing over her life and allow the Holy Spirit to minister in to this.

If you had looked closely during one of those refreshing meetings, you would have seen Irene waving her left hand up and down in a vigorous fashion. Without context, it looked odd, but with an awareness of what God had said to Irene, it was a release for her to be all God had called her to be. To say to all and everyone, 'I am who I am.'

'I'm Coming Home'

When John Shelbourne died, Stuart and Irene did all they could for the family but were left unsure as to what was best. It would not be a surprise for Muriel, John's widow, to feel unsure herself as to whether she could stay with new leaders when her own husband had been helping to lead previously.

Again, the Holy Spirit did a deep and wonderful work as part of the times of refreshing. During one of the meetings, Muriel was on the floor, having fallen under the power of the Spirt. She then began to do something rather odd. She started shouting 'Cooee, I'm coming home! Cooee, I'm coming home!'

Muriel was not one for extravagant or unusual behaviour, so Stuart was a little concerned.

On closer inspection, things appeared to be more concerning still.

Muriel had taken her shoes off and was banging them on the floor with her hands, at the same time as shouting she was coming home.

Odd behaviour, but Stuart had been in and around the Toronto Blessing long enough to know that what seemed strange may not be.

The meeting concluded and Stuart had not been able to catch Muriel and ask what had been happening. Muriel was able to share this with the whole church the week after.

The Holy Spirit had taken Muriel back to her childhood as she lay on the floor. As a child, coming home from school, she had to walk from the school bus, through a wooded area, to get to her house. To do this she needed wellingtons and took her shoes off to carry them. She would then shout, 'Cooee, I'm home!' to her mum and dad as she drew near to the house. Dad was the person who regularly came out to meet her.

As she was ministered to on the floor, she felt the Holy Spirit leading her through that childhood experience again. She again saw her dad come out of the house to meet her. And the Holy

Spirit brought comfort to her regarding the death of her father, which had been at an early age.

Then the Holy Spirit did the same thing for a second time. This time, He ministered to her regarding the death of her husband, John. As she came through the woodland, carrying her shoes and shouting her greeting, she opened her eyes and there were Stuart and Irene standing before her.

In one evening, the Holy Spirit had ministered love and grace over two traumatic deaths. And more than that, she knew she was in the right church with the right spiritual parents.

Muriel went on to serve for many years in the church, regularly teaching and preaching. Andrew Bell recalls that she was particularly supportive and encouraging towards him in that season.

Building

The 1990s was not just a time of building the church in terms of people, it was also a time of literal building. The building in the area of Newland, near the centre of the city of Lincoln, originated in 1840 and had been added to substantially in 1874, providing what was essentially two separate buildings next door to each other.

It goes without saying that with old buildings come ongoing costs. None more so than in the early 1990s when the congregation had to move out for three years in order for essential renovations to take place. Over £200,000 was raised by the church members to provide for these repairs, which included strengthening some of the foundations, some of which had been built on sandy soil. There was one additional change – the removal of the pews and the organ from downstairs.

Planning permission for the downstairs changes had been slow and challenging, but by 1994 the congregation were back in the building and celebrating not only the renovations but a new-found freedom from not being penned in by pews. Gerald Coates led the celebrations in September of that year in what was a joyous time of thanksgiving and worship.

University

As the church moved back into the building, Stuart and the team were particularly aware of a prophetic word they had received during their enforced absence from the building.

They'd had a visit from Dale Gentry, a prophetic minister living in Texas in the States. Dale was a friend of a friend and had connected with Stuart during a visit to the UK. At the time of his visit, he knew nothing at all about New Life Christian Fellowship, nor of Stuart and Irene.

This makes his prophetic words over the church more impactful.

At the time Dale was with them, Stuart and his leaders had been seriously considering giving up on the historic church buildings. The repair costs were coming in at a much higher figure than expected. The repairs were more difficult than at first thought. Maybe it would be best simply to move out to somewhere new and sell the buildings?

As Dale spoke during that Sunday service, he began to prophesy over the church. He spoke of the need to renovate the old buildings for the move of God that was intended and of the influence the church would have on the city and the nation subsequently. He said that the buildings were more important than the church realised. He spoke of a great move of the Spirit that would come to the students in the university at Lincoln as they attended the church in that building.

But there was a problem with the word. The city didn't have a university.

Just a few weeks after Dale's visit, the city authorities announced new plans. There was to be a university in Lincoln. Not only that but the site was to be on old industrial land just the other side of Brayford Pool, the waterway in front of Newland where the buildings stand.

The fruit of that prophetic word was not only the renovation of the buildings but the fact that over the years, many students from the university have found faith in Christ. A good number of the current staff at the church are ex-students from that university.

Turbulence

As in any Christian setting, it's not all prophetic blessing and growth. There's usually turbulence alongside blessing. It was Jonathan Edwards in the heat of revival in the First Great Awakening in the 1700s who said, 'There never yet was any great manifestation that God made of Himself to the world, without many difficulties attending it.'

The difficulties attending Stuart related to a painful shaking within his team, which led to a need for restructuring. This had a significant effect, not least upon work that needed to be covered both at the Lincoln church and with the fast-approaching Grapevine Celebration.

Caroline Cameron was by now working in the New Life offices. Starting as a volunteer, she had taken on a part-time role, helping to develop the teaching programme the church produced for new and future leaders.

As a result of the changes, Caroline had to step forward. As changes were being discussed, Irene walked over to Caroline, placed her hand on her shoulder and said the words, 'For such a time as this' (a reference to Esther's story in the Bible), and then walked off.

Caroline was soon to find out the significance of the comment. Thrown in at the deep end, she took on oversight of Grapevine, ensuring that the gaps created in its organisation were plugged. Her role developed further over time, working closely with Stuart on the broader strategy and oversight of Ground Level.

A Prophetic Edge

A super-organised individual, Caroline was responsible for helping Duane White when he came to the UK from the States for a period of six months of ministry (which lasted two years in the end). Duane and Kris White moved to Lincoln to help Stuart with the church. Upon his arrival in the office, Caroline was there to give him his schedule. As Duane recalls it, pretty much every day had meetings and ministry for the full six months. It felt a bit much at the time, but he began to appreciate the order and organisation that Caroline brought.

Duane's role in the church at Lincoln was to help and support Stuart and, in particular, to bring a prophetic edge to the church and to Ground Level.

His first encounter with Stuart had been just a few years earlier, meeting through a friend. Duane recalls Stuart's moderate manner – a sense that he was holding back – and Duane assumed this was a friendship that wouldn't last. But Stuart was simply being himself. Polite and cautious, maybe slightly reserved in how he deals with others, especially other leaders as he gets to know them.

But the friendship grew, particularly after Stuart observed the accuracy of Duane's prophetic ministry to some of his leaders. And with Duane and Kris feeling God was calling them to the UK for a while, the invite to join Stuart followed soon after.

Along the way, Stuart received an invite to travel to the States to work with Duane's churches and mission organisation there. That was when Duane introduced Stuart to Tony Miller. Tony's ongoing influence, particularly at Ground Level and Grapevine, can be seen from that time on, with his strong faith emphasis having a significant effect on the whole movement.

International

If you ask Stuart what he feels are the most significant links internationally, he will talk of Duane White in Texas, United States, of Jack and Trish Groblewski in Bethlehem, Pennsylvania, United States and of Louis and Natasja Kotzé in Hatfield, Pretoria, South Africa. Note the names come first, the churches and locations second. That's how it is. Always a relational leader, Stuart works with friends, not churches and positions. It makes for long-term involvement and the thrill of working together, not just in partnership, but in friendship.

Out of these relationships, others have flourished, particularly in the United States. Stuart meets regularly online with leaders in Pennsylvania, Virginia and Texas.

The link with the States came early and prophetically. At a leaders' conference organised by Gerald Coates, there was a prophetic word for Stuart, that he would be a bridge between the UK and the United States. Historically, there are strong links between Lincolnshire and the founding of America – something that Stuart and Jack Groblewski have studied further over the years.

It wasn't long afterwards when a whole team of leaders from the north-east seaboard of the States turned up at the Ground Level annual leaders' conference at Swanwick, Derbyshire. They had heard Stuart speaking in the States and there and then decided, as a church movement, they needed to be with Stuart and his leaders. It was during that conference that Pete Atkins spoke briefly about the Lincolnshire links with the States – the Puritans based at Gainsborough and Boston. John Smith, the founder of Jamestown in the early 1600s (and later romanticised in the Pocahontas story) also came from Lincolnshire.

His comments, as part of the notices, were almost in passing, but it was noticeable that a number of the American visitors were getting excited by what was being said. Pete spoke of the less than ideal approach of the British in early America and this again caused excitement. By the end of the session, a number were in tears. They had come with certain prejudices towards the British and Pete's kindly and apologetic approach had broken through, causing them to repent of that attitude.

Partners Without Ownership

What started that day in repentance towards each other's attitudes, developed into a close working relationship between the two networks.

Stuart was able to help considerably with the American network, and regularly spoke at their conferences. At one point the American brothers asked to become part of Ground Level. Stuart declined, arguing that they would be better as their own network, but that the two groups could work together, share resources and encourage each other. They could be partners without ownership – a phrase that has been developed by Stuart in a number of later relationships.

There are surely few apostolic leaders who would be able to turn down a request to join their network in the way that Stuart did.

Revival Centres

Stuart and Irene are particularly close to Jack and Trish Groblewski, often holidaying with them. Not that it started that way though.

Jack recalls being particularly 'off' with Stuart on his first visit to the States. Jack had been asked by Eddie Smith to invite Stuart over to preach. He declined to do so without listening first to a cassette or two of Stuart's teaching, in order to check him out. Eddie was not impressed and refused to send any cassettes, insisting that his word should be enough. Jack wouldn't budge.

With Stuart already in the States, Jack's father-in-law happened to be in a meeting where Stuart spoke, and reported back to Jack, insisting that he should have Stuart at their church. Jack still didn't move on it!

Eventually Jack relented but as he describes it, 'Stuart came in under a cloud of my own scrutiny!' At the end of the meeting Jack thanked Stuart, gave him a financial gift, and said 'goodbye', thinking that was that.

Two hours later, Jack's father-in-law came over to the house, along with Stuart, who he had been hosting for the rest of the day. Jack recalls thinking that he should at least be hospitable and invited them in.

As they chatted over coffee, Jack asked Stuart where he had been preaching. Stuart listed the five towns he had visited so far.

Suddenly, silence. Jack stared back at Stuart and asked him to repeat the names of the towns. They were fairly small places which would generally have been lost on a map of the United States. Jack fetched a map from his study. There were five towns circled on that map. The same five towns Stuart had preached in. The same five towns that Jack had felt impressed by the Holy Spirit to pray for in recent times. And so a friendship formed.

With children around the same age, it wasn't long before flights to and from the US and UK became annual events based around holidays.

As the children grew older, holidays without them became holidays with a purpose. Stuart and Irene, Jack and Trish began to visit old revival centres. They went to the places in New England where Jonathan Edwards and George Whitefield had preached in the 1700s, to Kentucky and the home of some of the Methodist Rider's revivals of the 1800s. In Europe, they visited the home of Nikolaus Zinzendorf, the supporter of the Moravian revivals. In the UK, there were visits to Epworth, the childhood home of John Wesley and to the places in London where Wesley and Whitefield had begun to preach in the open air – a practice that had been frowned upon by the established church of the day, but one which brought about the significant revival, referred to as the First Great Awakening in the UK and the US.

It was after the visit to Epworth that Stuart and Jack found themselves at Hull University, speaking to the students. They had been asked to speak about the baptism in the Holy Spirit. But they didn't get very far.

As Stuart began to speak about his own experience of the Holy Spirit, a student at the back cried out, 'Save me, oh God, save me!'

No sooner had they begun to pray for the young man than another student began to cry out. Across the room, young men and women under the conviction of the Holy Spirit began to call on God for mercy. There was a weight of conviction that night, not dissimilar to the experiences of the meetings of Wesley, Whitefield and Edwards in that first awakening. Jack describes it as God sending them a little post-card as to what it had been like in that awakening. Many found new life in Jesus Christ at that meeting. And Stuart and Jack never did get to preach.

Revival fascinates Stuart. There are no holidays separate from his cry for God to move again as of old. Each of these holiday visits would be surrounded in prayer. The 'Why not now, Lord?' prayer is never far from his lips.

Stuart actively seeks out revival. He's not afraid to get into the car or onto a plane to visit centres where the Holy Spirit is moving. Holy Spirit passion for God's presence means that the inconvenience of travel is no inconvenience at all.

More Fruit on the Vine

The influence of the Toronto Blessing had its effect on the Grapevine Celebration too. It had been called Grapevine because of the awareness as to where the nourishment came from. Churches would only be going through the motions were they to be separated from the vine. The kingdom purposes of God can only be accomplished when each church is receiving the goodness of God through a close walk with him. It's true for individuals. And it's true for churches too.

Grapevine was a declaration as to where the source was. Those attending were to hear from Him, receive, grow and share their faith.

With the impact of the Toronto Blessing on British shores, Grapevine became a source, too, for the outworking of the Holy Spirit, in ways already being witnessed elsewhere. Stuart welcomed this. He had already been a major catalyst in the UK and the USA and it was with a degree of excitement that he drove in to the showground in August 1995, expectant for what God would do.

Straight away, the outworking of the Holy Spirit on those gathered was clear. People falling to the ground. A weight of God's presence in the meetings. Jumping, screaming, shouting, shaking. And laughter. So much laughter. Waves of laughter across the congregation. Chris Bowater found it an easy thing to lead people in worship – they were almost ahead of him in anticipation as to what God would do and say.

'When the leadership of the worship transfers from the stage to the congregation it's special,' says Chris.

It was during one of these worship evenings that Chris had an impression in his mind that he should invite Martin Smith to the stage. At that time, Martin was working as a sound engineer and was in the outside sound van. Unknown as a musician outside a small network of friends, Martin had been writing songs for a while and had begun to privately record some with friends, under the name Cutting Edge. One song had stayed with Chris and it was this that came to mind during the evening worship in the big tent.

Getting up from his keyboard, Chris asked his friend Dave Hadden to take over.

'Martin, have you got your guitar with you?'

'Sure. Why?'

'I want you to sing on the main stage. That song you were playing the other day. Can you do it?'

That night, an unknown worshipper stood with his acoustic and sang as the Holy Spirit ministered.

Thank You for saving me, what can I say?

You are my everything, I will sing Your praise

You shed Your blood for me, what can I say?

You took my sin and shame

A sinner called by name

Great is the Lord

Great is the Lord

For we know Your truth has set us free

You've set Your hope in me

Martin J Smith © 1993 Curious? Music UK (Admin by Integrity Music www. IntegrityRights.com)

There was a hush in the tent. Many were in tears. Such a sense of God's love.

At the end of the song, Martin continued to play and began to sing prophetically. 'Lord, whatever happens to me, I will always serve You...' Prophetic indeed. That night, as Martin drove home, he was in a car crash and almost lost his life. Those gathered at Grapevine prayed. God saved.

Beyond Limitations

As the event had expanded and moved from the exhibition halls to a hired big-top, the network expanded too. More churches linked up with Ground Level. Stuart was invited further afield to teach and preach. In a sense, the event itself was impacting well beyond the limitations of the week and well beyond the teaching during that week.

Key to this were the ongoing communications both from Grapevine and from Ground Level. *Grapevine News*, the newspaper produced for each Grapevine event, covered the programme for the week as well as a number of articles relating to what was happening. Stuart used this as a platform to inform and challenge the churches, one hand pointing upwards and the other outwards to all that was happening with Ground Level and the related churches.

Gerald Coates was open handed in his support for Stuart and in 1996 he invited Stuart to join him on board *Compass Magazine*. To that point, the magazine had been for Pioneer churches, but it then opened up as a joint publication, incorporating Ground Level. The joint editorship of a Christian magazine speaks to the closeness of relationship between Stuart and Gerald. The magazine began during the Toronto Blessing and there is a strong emphasis on the work of the Holy Spirit throughout its run. Here is Stuart in the first joint issue, defending the Toronto Blessing:

Evangelicals often have predetermined expectations with regard to revival that don't include laughter, shaking and aerobics! The fruit can be seen. But many get stuck at the phenomena and don't stay around very long to observe further . . . Giving God room is essential, as we soon revert back to the safety of programmes and routines. There's something in British Church life that emphasises activity . . . [but] I'm not sure we're looking for 'business as usual'. Our desire is to see a totally new dimension of God break into every area of our lives.

The growing influence and open doors Stuart was witnessing at this time is reflected in his diary. *Link-up*, the Ground Level newsletter for Autumn 1998, records Stuart speaking or participating at a number of national conferences, an apostolic leaders' day, an international conference, Ground Level days, a regional leaders' conference and a number of individual churches. This is on top of his oversight of the Lincoln church. As Stuart records in the *Compass Magazine* article, it may not be 'business as usual' but it is certainly busy!

Stuart was busy writing as well. In 1998, at the request of the US publishing company Destiny Image, Stuart wrote *In Search of Revival*. This records Stuart's own experiences during the early days of the Toronto Blessing, accompanied by biblical teaching on revival. This was followed in 2003 with *Rebuilding the Walls*, an in-depth study of the books of Ezra and Nehemiah and its application to the Church of today.

His book *Rebuilding the Walls* includes within it an appendix which, by way of example for church growth, shows the vision of Ground Level. Stuart iterates the objective of 'a cell in every village, a congregation in every town and a celebration in the city from the Humber to the Wash'. The strategy follows – prayer, research, equipping and planting, with a special emphasis on training young people. By 1996 Stuart was working with Pete Atkins who had a clear strategy for reaching rural villages in that same region. By 2002 a specific Church Planting School had been established to help train more leaders within Ground Level.

Ground Level was keen to reflect compassion ministries in their approach to church growth, none more so than with their relationship to Betel Ministries. Betel started on the streets of Madrid in 1985 and has grown into a worldwide ministry in twenty-seven countries, helping homeless and drug- and alcohol-dependent individuals. Led by Elliott Tepper, Betel's intention is not just to help addicts but to build future leaders – apostles, prophets, pastors and teachers among them. The synergy to Stuart and his work with Ground Level is an obvious one. Churches have started as a result and the UK Betel churches are part of Ground Level.

The outworking of the Toronto Blessing and its impact upon Stuart has been reflected in a logical, steady process of building church – something at which Stuart excels. The dynamic of the Holy Spirit must be reflected in a growing church. The experience of the believer has to be rooted in further Christian salvations, church growth and kingdom extension. Always disciplined, always seeking to run steadily to the rhythm of the Holy Spirit, Stuart caught hold of the move of the Spirit and with positive and practical application, applied it to a growing church and church movement.

Chapter Nine
The Turn Of A Page

As the 2002 Grapevine Celebration began, Stuart and Irene sat at the back of the bleachers, looking out on the empty big-top in front of them, soon to be filled with thousands of people. What a privilege to lead this celebration. How amazing to work in partnership with so many men and women within Ground Level. How good God has been in caring for the family – all three children following God, in good health, and local to Lincoln. It was as if their lives were covered in gold dust. Such blessing. Such protection. Such a work of the Holy Spirit. Such a good God.

And this year at Grapevine looked to be especially good. Record numbers: 12,000 in 2002. With the closure of the Stoneleigh Bible Week led by Newfrontiers, many had come instead to Grapevine.

Who would have guessed that in rural Lincolnshire, God would move in such a way and through an event they had faithfully carried over the years?

The teaching as always would be great, the worship exceptional. Even though it was now a big event, it had kept the family feel. And it was with thankfulness that Stuart and Irene sat there that evening before the start of the event. Grateful hearts for all God had done.

'I wonder,' said Stuart, 'if moments like this of refreshing and blessing are there to prepare us for harder days? You know, Irene, like Joseph – the days of plenty providing for the challenging years that followed. Perhaps we are meant to store up all of the goodness we have enjoyed to help us face more difficult days?'

It wasn't meant as a prophetic statement. But it may as well have been.

Health and Family

The page had been turned. From times of refreshing to times of trial. Yes. Just like Joseph. Days of plenty to days of famine. Challenge, upheaval and sickness.

Over those years, all of Stuart and Irene's four parents died. Their greatest supporters. The ones who held on when others were saying it wouldn't work. The faithful ones. The giving ones.

It was a hard lesson in believing God's goodness and grace, in trusting in the hardest of times.

Not long afterwards, Irene began to struggle with excruciating back pains. The problem remained undiagnosed as Grapevine approached. The only way for Irene to get there would be with the use of a wheelchair. Not the best of pictures to present at a faith camp, but better than missing it.

Early on in the week, an orthopaedic surgeon who was a member of one of the Ground Level churches, spotted Irene and asked if he could examine her back.

The diagnosis was swift. And the prognosis was not good without immediate surgery. Irene ended up having major back surgery with bars and screws fitted. But without the surgeon, it would have been so much worse.

And then came Dave.

Eye Trouble

Their youngest son, Dave, began to complain of an eye problem early in 2003. He described his right eye as a bit 'sleepy' on occasions and there was a little bit of a droop to the eyelid.

At sixteen, the baby of the family by about ten years, Dave had grown up loving church, loving music, loving football, loving practical jokes . . . and adoring Grapevine. 'Better than Christmas except for the divine birth bit' was his jokey comment. He'd never been seriously ill.

A referral to a specialist eye unit at Leicester Royal Infirmary followed. Both Dave and Stuart were in good spirits as they arrived. Some kind of dark mass had shown at the back of the right eye in an earlier scan and both were putting it down to internal swelling from a clash of heads at a recent football match.

A biopsy was carried out. The surgeon at the Leicester hospital got straight to the point.

'I am almost certain it's cancer.'

Silence. What do you say when you hear these words? Stuart swallowed hard. Dave was still under the anaesthetic. What to say when he wakes?

Stuart is honest as Dave comes round: 'He's found something he doesn't like.'

Dave takes it calmly at first, but when you're sitting in a hospital bed with little else you can do, thinking takes over. Panic takes over.

A quick discussion with Dad, and Duane and Kris White are called for. Nowadays back in Texas, at the time they were helping Stuart in Lincoln. A two-hour journey sees them arrive at Leicester Royal. Prayers are prayed, comfort given.

Dave is visibly shaken. As he walks Duane and Kris to the lift in the hospital, he stops and looks at them.

'One of the questions on the hospital form was to ask whether I have godparents. I wonder. Would you guys be my godparents?'

A poignant moment. An emotional moment.

Throughout Dave's illness, Duane and Kris stay close. Duane recalls many a McDonald's milkshake with Dave as the weeks went by, talking, helping, praying, supporting.

'Duane, do you think I'm going to die?'

'Dave, we're all going to die. I don't think that now is your time but I can't really answer that question.'

'Do you have a prophetic word for me, Duane?'

'No, I don't have a specific word from God. But I do have *the* Word of God. I will help you. I will teach you faith, I will give you a theology for faith. I will teach you how to believe God for healing. And we can walk together that way.'

The next week is one of the darkest of Dave's life. What Dave describes as the terror of the unknown. As a boy he had feared losing his sight. And here was the moment. As a boy, Dave had feared losing his hair. And, again, here was the moment.

The diagnosis was that it was a rare and aggressive cancer, but that was a good thing in a way as chemotherapy would be the best weapon. Surgery would not be needed. Sight could be saved.

Call David's Mighty Men

Stuart wrestled with what to do. Believing in God's direct healing as well as through the surgeon's hand, Stuart was keen not to dismiss any method of healing and that included chemotherapy.

He felt to pray. In fact he heard God give him a prayer strategy – to call together David's mighty men. In the Old Testament, before David is made king in Jerusalem, he gathers mighty men around him, ready for the fight.

This David too – David Bell of Lincoln, England – would also have his mighty men and women. Prayer warriors, called together for a purpose. That purpose being wholeness and healing.

Stuart chose carefully. Telephone calls were made. A special meeting was arranged. Each man and woman represented prayer warriors ready for a fight. There was no room for doubt. No room for 'what if?'. This was a call to war. To defeat the very real enemy of cancer. To defeat the evil spirit behind it. The call was to pray and to continue to pray. Like David's mighty men of old, to break through in the purposes of God and see complete victory, complete healing.

During that long first week from diagnosis, prayer warriors gathered every night.

At the first gathering, Stuart counted the number. Thirty. Thirty prayer warriors. The exact number of David's mighty men. Stuart hadn't planned it that way. There were more than thirty on the list. But that was the number that first evening.

And then, remarkably, thirty on the second night. And the third . . . Different people came on different nights. But each night, exactly thirty gathered.

On the final prayer night, Stuart counted again. Twenty-nine. Ah, well, never mind. Maybe it wasn't a God thing after all. Just an overactive imagination. And then, as they started to pray, one more person came through the door.

'Sorry I'm late!'

Wow. It was as if God was underlining the call to prayer. And if He was emphasising and confirming that prayer aspect, then how much more a confirmation that Dave would be healed?

Each night they prayed, declared, prophesied the victory of God. One saw in a picture Dave standing as a grown man with a wife and children. The picture was taken up by the whole group, prayed through, battled for. There were some serious breakthroughs in heavenly places that week.

Prayers prayed. Prophecies delivered. Scriptures declared:

And this is the confidence that we have towards him, that if we ask anything according to his will he hears us. And if we know that he hears us in whatever we ask, we know that we have the requests that we have asked of him. (1 John 5:14-15)

The Gold Underneath

After that first week, the group committed to meet weekly on a Sunday night and to continue until there was breakthrough.

Jeff Lucas was an observer of that group:

They fought like mad in prayer, but never slipped into unreality. It was tenacious faith married to reality. The quality of those prayer times reminded me of the three young men in Daniel in the Bible. Their approach was that 'God is able to heal – but even if He doesn't, we will still praise Him'.

Pete Atkins was one of that praying group. As a GP, he was more aware than most of the journey Dave had to take. Aware, too, of the toll it could take on the parents, Pete recalls the pressure on Stuart and Irene:

The pressure he and Irene were under was immense. We wanted to do our best as a prayer team. I was aware of the medical possibilities with Dave but wanted to remain positive for the family – we all did. We kept the word of God at the front of our praying and our declaration in that season. Standing on the promises of words that God gave. Avoiding the glib comments but always speaking in faith. As a prayer group, we all needed to walk carefully before God. It wasn't easy – it was warfare. It was a pressured time but also a precious time.

As the family fought in prayer, as the church cried out, as Christian friends around the world committed to pray, it took its toll on Stuart physically. As a GP, Pete saw what was happening.

I've never seen Stuart any worse than at that time. He lost weight. He looked physically shrunken by the pressure of it all. But at the same time, he continued to believe, to pray, to lead. It's at moments like these – life-changing moments – that you see the real person. You see the gold underneath.

Ward 27

Chemotherapy. A cruel word. Little that reflects therapy. And a lot that reflects pain.

But if God wants to heal that way, He can heal that way.

It was hard settling into Ward 27. The children's oncology ward at Leicester Royal.

Test after test. Procedure after procedure. Including a visit to the sperm bank. Jeff Lucas is in town. A well-known Christian speaker and author and a long-term friend of the Bell family. He and Stuart join Dave on the trek over to the sperm bank.

This is a tricky one. A sixteen-year-old boy has just been told that the chemo may make him infertile. So just to be sure, save some sperm in the meantime.

It could be embarrassing. But Jeff is the perfect person to be there. Unpretentious. Occasionally absurd. Loud. And completely genuine. A passion and a compassion combined that meant his presence in the waiting room was a gift from a good God who knew exactly what Dave needed at that moment.

As Dave reappears from a side room, clasping a small container, he waves it in the air, shouting 'Victory!' Jeff and Dad stand to their feet cheering. It's fair to say the rest of those in the clinic have a look of complete bemusement on their faces.

Jeff recalls arriving that day with a bottle of champagne. He felt he had heard God tell him to buy the bottle and to put it on the mantlepiece in Stuart and Irene's home. As Jeff explains, 'This was not meant as an assurance of a successful outcome but as a reminder to the family that there would be a day when they would celebrate again.'

That moment in the sperm bank is one of the better ones in those first few weeks. As the Hickman line is fitted via an operation to the top of Dave's heart to administer the drugs, things get serious.

Sickness. Severe vomiting. The feeling of not being there, as if in a dream. And then the reality again. More vomiting.

And hair loss. On a visit home, brother-in-law Glen gets out the shaving equipment to remove the bits that are left.

Mud in the Eye

It would be wonderful to say that after the trauma of the chemo, that was it. But it wasn't. Radiotherapy followed.

All through this time, the faithful prayed. Stuart and Irene in particular of course. Stuart had felt God say that Dave's healing would come in a similar way to the story of Naaman in the Old Testament. He had to wash himself in the muddy Jordan River seven times to be healed. Why not clean water once? Why the mud? It reminded Stuart of the time Jesus healed a blind man by spitting and rubbing mud in his eye. Not the most obvious way to bring healing.

But for Dave, this was to be the way. The journey was a muddy one. An emotional one. Talk to Stuart and Irene about it today, and the tears are still there. Deep and raw emotions played their part in this particular journey.

On one occasion in a leaders' meeting organised by Gerald Coates, each leader was asked to share one point for prayer. When it came to Stuart, he was overcome with emotion. The room knew why. Dave Carr, a well-known minister from Birmingham, walked over to Stuart and with the words, 'This is what God feels,' Dave began to cry, hugging Stuart and kissing him on the forehead.

So many prayed. Leaders across the country sent words of encouragement and prophecy. If they were to be listed, it would look like a 'who's who' of the apostolic and prophetic networks of the UK. So many prayers. So many words.

And then a day.

Stuart was in a leaders' meeting arranged by Terry Virgo when it happened. He and Irene were awaiting the final results from the latest set of scans. His mobile began to ring. Rushing out of the room, Stuart took the call. Irene was on the line. In amongst the sobs and tears, she was able to say seven words that changed their lives:

'There is no evidence of any disease.'

For the family, for the church, for Stuart and his own ministry, this had been a battle. Probably the hardest one he and Irene have ever had to fight.

But there was only ever going to be one victor. Jesus Christ.

The Postscript

There's another story here.

In 2022, a lump was identified on Dave's neck. It turned out to be entirely benign and unrelated to the earlier condition. But it still needed to be removed. Britain's NHS was still recovering from the hit from Covid so the waiting list was long, despite the advice to get the lump removed as soon as possible.

Friends in America came to the rescue. They were able to identify and finance an operation in the United States and the successful operation went ahead.

On their return from the States, Stuart and Dave went to Chroma Church in Leicester. It was a church in revival and Dave received some powerful ministry on that night.

As they were leaving that evening, Stuart asked how far the church building was from Leicester Royal Infirmary.

'Oh, less than a mile – it's just there, over the road.'

How appropriate that the final words on Dave's illness should be prayed and declared in the same place it started.

And remember that prophetic picture from the time the prayer warriors gathered? Dave standing as a grown man with a wife and children?

Today, it's true.

Chapter Ten
The Testing And The Trials

Heavy rain and camping don't go well together. The rain had been incessant up until the start of Grapevine 2004. Nevertheless, as the week began, the clouds cleared.

Catastrophe

The evening of Sunday 29th August 2004 started with worship in the big tent. Around three thousand had gathered as Martin Smith from Delirious? led the worship. He encouraged everyone there to hold hands – and to dance.

It was the second instruction that resulted in an evening that will not be forgotten. But for the wrong reasons.

As people danced and jumped in worship, there was a crack. A scream. More screams. Shouts for help.

As people turned around in the main blocks of seats, they could see what had happened. A whole section of the bleachers had collapsed.

These wooden stands, built up near the back of the tent, were several rows high. Looking from the stage, the section on the right had fallen.

And so had the people on that section.

Glen, Stuart's son-in-law, was in charge of everything to do with the main tent that year, as Site Director. In fact he had taken the role on for the first time. That evening, Glen and Becki were both off duty and sitting in the main block.

Glen could see what had happened and leapt into action. Despite the possible dangers of further collapse, Glen jumped over the chairs and ran down under the fallen bleachers.

It was surreal. Effectively he was looking for bodies, checking with each person that they were alive and aware of their surroundings. One to another, one to another. Stay still. Don't move. Help is coming. Yes, you're going to be okay.

By now, an off-duty police officer had found a megaphone and was shouting to people to stay where they were, not to try to move.

Stuart and Irene had been near the front of the meeting. As the realisation hit as to what happened, Stuart too went to the back. By now someone was on the main stage microphone, instructing everyone out of the tent and back to their campsites. The instruction was to stay calm and to pray. Emergency services had been called, all would be well.

Off-duty doctors and nurses began to attend to the wounded where they lay under the stands. Chris Bowater's daughter Rachel was among them. Newly qualified as a doctor, she quickly began to set up drips, administering drugs to those most in pain. A senior casualty registrar also happened to be there that night who was able to bring support and direction.

All the Bell family remember what they were doing at the moment they heard. Becki was in the meeting with Glen, of course. She immediately looked to Mum and Dad at the front, aware of what they would be going through as they took in the scene. Becki remembers a few leaders dropping to their knees in prayer. And then the concern for Glen as he ran into the danger area.

Andrew had been working in the 12s-to-14s children's venue when news reached him. His immediate thoughts were whether Mum and Dad were safe. Then to what to do with the children in his meeting. Andrew is prone to over-analyse, but that evening he felt God's presence in being immediately able to work out solutions for children whose parents may not collect them, through to telling the kids what was happening in an acceptable way.

Dave had been helping in the youth venue. Aware that Dad was going to make an announcement, he and others were listening in to the Grapevine radio station for more information and instructions.

One story that found its way into the public domain from that evening relates to a lady who was unsure as to whether to respond to Martin Smith's encouragement to hold the hand of the person next to her and dance. It wasn't the kind of thing she usually did. But the man next to her on the bleachers encouraged her to do so.

That decision saved her. As her stand collapsed, the man next to her, on the next set of bleachers, was able to keep hold of her as she fell, pulling her up to safety.

Stuart was approached by one of his leaders who also happened to be a lawyer. Stuart was encouraged not to say too much publicly and the two of them prepared the words that were read out over the radio that evening.

In the meantime, a fleet of ambulances began to arrive. The county had declared it as a critical event and already news had reached the local radio station.

A tent was repurposed for the walking wounded and pretty much every doctor and nurse on site volunteered to help.

An hour or two later, after the initial shock, found Stuart and Irene at the hospital, talking and praying with those who had been brought in. Most were discharged the same evening, although there were a couple of more serious injuries, especially a lady who suffered a severe leg wound.

The American TV news channel CNN got hold of the story at some point. They calculated, based on the numbers at the event, numbers on the bleachers and the fall of over twelve feet for some from those bleachers, how many fatalities there would be. Their calculated number is lost now, but the actual number that died? None.

Contingencies

One of the main messages that night was that the well-prepared contingency plans for an emergency event worked completely.

The day before, Glen, new to the job of Site Director, had decided to extend the entrance area to give more access. That decision meant that ambulances were able to drive right into the tent to the affected area.

Other contingencies kicked in as well. The rest of the week was to go ahead. Because the tent would be an investigation area for the police, the smaller tents were turned into main venues, with meetings running back-to-back in multiple sites and speakers moving from one to the other to teach and preach.

The very next morning after the catastrophe, an open-air meeting was called, with those attending thanking God for His mercies. The final meeting of the event was held in the youth venue but the weather was good enough for chairs to be placed outside as well, so everyone was able to attend. Gratitude and thanks became the theme of the week. In fact, the very first sermon from the main stage before the bleachers had collapsed had been from Jack Groblewski. Jack had felt to preach on the whole issue of gratitude and thanks. He had questioned at the time as to whether he had heard God's direction on that, as it didn't seem to be a particularly dynamic topic. But with the collapse of the bleachers, the reason for the theme became clear.

The week was a long one for Stuart. Feeling the pressure of leadership, he was grateful for Jeff Lucas being there. One of the speakers that year, Jeff made sure he stayed close to Stuart and Irene as the week went on, just being there as a friend. And he was needed. It may not have been noticeable to everyone, but all three children could see the effect the accident had on their parents. To carry a Bible Week at the best of times and in the best of weather is a significant responsibility. To have to carry a week when there has been a major accident is just hard.

Stuart and Irene look back on that time with thanksgiving. No loss of life. Few serious injuries. A commendation from both the police and the ambulance service on the processes in place for an emergency. And a wonderful generosity from those attending. Not only from those with medical expertise helping, but also in the final offering of the week for mission. It was the most generous amount ever given at Grapevine.

The investigation noted that there had been heavy rainfall the weeks before the tent and bleachers were erected. Their conclusion was that no one was culpable, and no charges were made. It was what might be called in insurance circles an 'act of God'. Somewhat ironic in the circumstances.

Tired and emotional, Stuart and Irene returned home grateful for God's mercy.

The next year, Stuart ensured that the first person to lead worship in the big-top was Martin Smith.

Listening and Supporting

It was because of crises such as this that a leaders' prayer group was set up. This consisted of a small number with clear apostolic ministry and included both Stuart and Jeff Lucas. Someone nicknamed it 'the generals' meeting' – a label those involved are quick to point out was not what they themselves had christened the group.

Jeff remembers meeting a man at Spring Harvest in France who said that he had a word for him. The word was 'you need to meet as generals again'. And so, the group continued with a new energy.

As always as leaders, such groups are so precious. To be able to share on a confidential basis with leaders in similar situations is both a privilege and a lifesaver.

This gathering also brought something of a shared voice in ministry. Jeff recalls following Stuart around the UK to a number of different events and larger churches, to find that he had spoken on the same subject Jeff intended to speak on.

Another leadership grouping that has been important to Stuart over the years has been the Partners For Influence network of apostolic leaders. This started with Stuart in the UK and Jack in the States. Later, a strong connection with South Africa developed. It is fair to say that Stuart helped stabilise the South Africa church when one of the key leaders stepped down.

One of the members of Partners For Influence is Dave Smith of KingsGate Church, Peterborough. The church, which has four campuses, numbers about 2,000 in terms of attendance and has its own purpose-built auditorium in Peterborough, which has an eventual seating capacity of 1,800. Dave has come to appreciate Stuart as a friend, mentor and as one KingsGate's long-standing apostolic advisors.

Trials, Tests and Tornadoes

The bleachers catastrophe was not the first challenge for Grapevine. One year a tornado ripped through the site, turning over caravans and blowing one man up into a tree. The main tent was hit and was collapsed down to its lower emergency level, surviving the day.

A test of a different kind came when Gerald Coates was one of the main speakers. Gerald is always controversial and has a particular dislike for religiosity. He had spoken to a magazine and appeared to indicate he may not believe in the inerrancy of scripture. Stuart wanted to give Gerald the opportunity to put things straight in a late-night interview at Grapevine.

But he didn't take that opportunity. On the contrary, he seemed to again suggest the Bible was not inerrant.

A number from the Assemblies of God executive team were there that night. And they were there to try and catch Gerald out, having read the original article. It appeared that Gerald played into their hands.

At the end of the interview, Stuart ran to the back where the recordings of the meetings were being produced.

'Please don't put that one out. We'll not produce that one as a resource.'

'I'm sorry, Stuart, it's already out.'

It seemed as though the Assemblies of God executive members in attendance had what they wanted. Condemning proof that Gerald was a heretic. Some challenged Stuart to disown him and his comments.

Stuart wouldn't do so.

'Gerald is my friend. He has stood by me so many times in the past. I won't disown him now.'

The pressure was intense. The recording was sent around a number of churches. A church in the Shetlands left Ground Level. Stuart wondered how much his ministry would be affected, but he wouldn't speak on it and, in the end, the Assemblies of God moved on to other things.

For the record, Gerald was not a heretic, and he did believe in the authority of scripture. But he did like to stir up controversy, especially when he perceived people were playing at religion rather than pursuing Christ. Was he aware of the Assemblies of God executive in the room that night? Did he sense there were 'religious' people there to try and trip him up? Quite possibly.

It's rare that Stuart is challenged on theology himself. He has been called the 'non-threatening radical' and someone who radically holds to the middle ground. Plus he is just so likeable! It's hard to pick a fight with someone who comes over as gracious and sincere, someone who is passionate for all God would have for His Church, but who is also able to discern the difference between a work of the Holy Spirit and a fad of the moment. It has served him well.

Betrayal

If you're on a main stage as a Christian, sooner or later you will get shot at. This has happened for Stuart less than for others because of his gentle manner, but it does happen.

Dave's battle with cancer and the bleachers collapsing are the two moments that immediately come to mind were you to ask Stuart and Irene about stressful moments, but there are two more that in a way run deeper. And that's because they concern betrayal, people within the church deliberately wanting to bring discord.

One Monday morning, staff arrived in the offices to find that the church's bank accounts had been frozen.

Payments couldn't be made, staff couldn't be paid.

Two leaders within the church had decided that if the church were to leave Assemblies of God whilst a few members wanted to remain connected, these members were legally entitled to the assets and the buildings. This action was particularly disturbing to John Phillips, who was at the time a member of the executive council of the Assemblies of God. John found it hard to believe that conversations had taken place behind his back and that legal advice had been sought without him knowing.

It appeared that the legal position was that a handful of people who wanted to remain in Assemblies of God could genuinely be the owners of all the assets. Stuart knew that this was particularly painful for the two Johns and suggested that rather than the church being taken to court, they should make a gift to the small group, allowing them to continue to be connected to Assemblies of God. It was a choice – either money from the church or a possible legal battle. £50,000 was sent to the group to allow the purchase of their original small building in the south of the city.

Interestingly, today, the church that now own that building are good friends of Stuart and Irene.

The second betrayal happened in 2011 when Stuart was approaching his sixtieth birthday and the family wanted to celebrate. Dave, with the encouragement of Paul Benger and Duane White, felt that it would be good to put on some kind of church event by way of a 'thank you' for all the faithful years of service. It was important, of course, that Dad didn't know what was happening.

They were thinking big. One of the rooms on the Lincolnshire Showground. Invitations to people all over the country – all those who were close to Stuart and Irene. Some video commendations for those who couldn't make it. A big meal.

Sounds good.

The invitations went out inviting people to the event and to help contribute towards a gift.

It looked as though this was the moment that a few in the church had been waiting for. A small number had never really accepted Stuart as the leader of the church and now was a good time to say so. They assumed that Dave was intending to use church money to fund Stuart's birthday celebration, and that Dave had also used the church database to get the word out. Neither were true but it didn't stop the accusation.

Stuart was away travelling at the time this happened. By the time he got back, a hand-delivered 'private and confidential' letter had been placed in all three of Stuart and Irene's children's hands. And the original letter – in the obligatory brown envelope – was awaiting Stuart's return.

'Dear Stuart, on your return from your travels, you will by

now have found that you will have a bigger surprise than your forthcoming birthday . . .'

The letter went on to list a number of issues, all of them untrue or exaggerated, with the main points relating to Dave organising the birthday event.

Andrew remembers the moment they met to discuss it – Stuart and Irene asked all three children to breakfast at McDonald's. There was genuine shock over what had been done. All five were in tears that morning.

The protagonists had written to the Charity Commission requesting an investigation. The Commission were actually very helpful and assured Stuart that this kind of thing happened all the time. There was no need to worry, but they would need to investigate.

Questionnaires went out to the trustees to complete and appropriate questions were asked. The trustees felt obliged to take legal advice and had a meeting with a Christian lawyer to establish what could be done.

In the end, the Charity Commission concluded that no money had gone out from the church and that the church database had not been used. The finances were all in order and a clean bill of health resulted.

The party was cancelled anyhow, and a smaller celebration arranged.

The harm was emotional. For people who Stuart had worked with and had trusted to go behind his back to the Charity Commission. For them to single out Dave for accusations of misuse of money and databases. For letters to have gone out to the family. For gossip to have gone around the church. These things hurt. Unfounded accusations are always the hardest to deal with.

And in the end, the truth comes out. A clean bill of health from the Charity Commission.

A few years later, in 2016, Stuart was awarded the British Empire Medal (BEM) from the late Queen. This recognised the work in the community throughout Lincolnshire by a number of churches and congregations. Without Stuart knowing at the time, he was put forward for this award by the local Member of Parliament, the Bishop of Lincoln and a member of the County Council. The award was presented by the Lord Lieutenant of Lincolnshire on behalf of Her Majesty the Queen. And perhaps even more excitingly, Stuart and Irene got to go to the Queen's garden party at Buckingham Palace.

And maybe as well there was a God-recognition in that award, for a man of passion and integrity, someone who has overcome malice and gossip with a good dose of grace and compassion. And someone with the ability to keep running, to keep the main thing the main thing.

Stuart missed his seventieth birthday celebration as well, due to the Covid lockdown. So, if anyone wants to organise a party . . . just saying.

Chapter Eleven
Heritage

Now in their seventies, Stuart and Irene want to finish well. They are still fully active within Alive Church and with Ground Level there are outline plans in place to hand on the baton. This is not a hard thing for them – all their Christian lives have been used to help disciple others, to bring through the next generation.

Despite their good health, Stuart and Irene are aware of the frailties of age. The sadness in recent years of losing big brother Graham to cancer makes the awareness sharper still. Graham was one of the biggest supporters of all Stuart and Irene did and was particularly involved in prophetic ministry into the churches. A fighter to the last, even in the final stages of cancer he made it to a Ground Level leaders' conference.

So yes, there's an awareness. If anything, this has sharpened the ministry further. They already have a heritage. And they plan to create more of one.

Ground Level Transition

Stuart felt it was important not to change the leadership of their church and Ground Level at the same time. Hence, the

Ground Level changes have largely taken place, but the change in leadership at church is at a slower pace. Eventually, Stuart and Irene will move to the role of Founding Pastors, with new senior leaders in place.

April 2020 saw Paul and Jeannie Benger move alongside Stuart and Irene in order to take over the leadership of Ground Level. Paul and Jeannie lead IKON Church based in Chesterfield, with five campuses reaching towns and cities in the locality. Stuart and Irene remain part of the Ground Level team which nowadays is quite extensive, including around thirty-five people responsible for various aspects of running this growing model of church life.

The transition has worked well. Stuart invited Paul to work alongside him, training him in the overall leadership, and then has led with him jointly for a while, before finally releasing Paul to take the lead – the final phase still to happen at the time of writing. Ultimately, Stuart and Irene will take on an ambassadorial role for the group.

Historically, leaders of church networks and apostolic groups have often found it hard to let go. Pete Atkins recognises a gift within Stuart that allows him to not only encourage leaders but see them replace him in different roles, often seeing future leadership in someone before others do. He is not afraid to give away when he sees the kingdom need to do so. His passion for the Church is greater than any personal ambition. Surely, part of an apostolic gift is to see the greater cause. That may be an obvious thing to say of any church leader, but history points to difficult transitions and even the break-up of movements where a leader has stayed too long.

The Three Cs

In the early 2010s, New Life Christian Fellowship became Alive Church. The new name reflected a change in the way the local church was constructed.

Instead of having one large congregation, the decision was taken to move to more of a 'campus' model – one church but numerous congregations. What is sometimes called 'multi-site church'. There would still be room for the celebration meetings when everyone came together at the central Lincoln building, but for the rest of the time, the congregations would work separately with their own leadership. That leadership would, though, still be linked to one central structure.

Stuart and Irene would continue to lead, with one hand on the tiller and the other waving forward other younger leaders to take up the steering.

The model has a further layer to it – the cell group or life group. Members of Alive are therefore part of a midweek accountability group, part of a Sunday congregation and part of something bigger, expressed in monthly celebrations when all come together. The celebration once a month has proved important for presenting that bigger picture as to what is happening, and Stuart would be the main speaker at most of these.

Cell, congregation, celebration – the three Cs.

Alive Growth

The proof of the model has been a growth in church planting and church membership. Traditionally within the movement, planting a new church was a rather laborious exercise, but a multi-site approach allows for a swifter growth. Young leaders may well feel more equipped to run a campus or location than to be launched out into a responsibility for a separate church without the closeness of other leaders and pastors.

The first three sites were Central Lincoln, South Lincoln and Grantham. Already the new structure was allowing for a congregation in another town entirely, which was an exciting move.

All of this has allowed for growth without the pressure of one large congregation in one large building. At the time of writing, there are now seven different locations, all part of Alive Church.

But not all the same. This is no 'Starbucks model' with all locations reflecting the same feel, the same preaching and the same worship style. Each reflects the local leadership. This has also helped with church outreach, with each location able to run an Alpha Course or other model, reflective of the community around them. Add to that an awareness of what is needed with local community support through compassion ministries such as a food bank, and this local flexibility, whilst retaining an overall direction of travel, has worked well.

Within the Lincoln locations, their compassion model is called Acts Trust. Separate from the church in order to more easily operate as a charity within the city, it is still very much part of Alive Lincoln. Acts Trust offers support to single mothers, special needs children, out-of-hours care, those needing financial help and advice, and more. There is a food bank and a newly created grocery store, in partnership with the Message Trust. The café at Alive Church, born out of the final piece of building work when the two separate buildings were joined through a covered courtyard, is run by Betel charity, but again it is very much part of the church outreach and compassion ministries.

The Covid pandemic forced a further change on the larger

locations in terms of church members meeting. They have each broken down further into communities, which proved to be a helpful way of keeping in touch during lockdown and the times thereafter. The key words during the pandemic for Alive Church were 'family' and 'relationship', and this was achieved through the additional structure.

The smaller units with the bigger vision have enabled locations to enjoy central men's and women's conferences and central support for leadership training.

An exciting additional part of the growing Alive model is a new television slot on Trinity Broadcasting Network (TBN) each Sunday evening for twelve weeks.

Magnetism

The picture at Alive Church and Ground Level is one of health and unity. These are hard to achieve where in many church situations, poor communication leads to gossip and infighting. There has been a share of that, particularly with regard to the betrayals at the Lincoln church.

And that has hurt.

Stuart and Irene dealt with it well but it has left them a bit vulnerable. Close friends comment that they can be a little insecure in their relationships with their fellow leaders and there is support and affirmation for them in helping to overcome that weakness. Was it always there? Possibly. Being a leader can be lonely. Inviting friends into confidences and seeing those confidences betrayed has left its mark on what may already have been a weakness.

One potential outworking of that insecurity can be the appointment of leaders in the same image as the senior leader.

The less insecurity, the broader the leadership base and the wider the style. At times when it has been needed, close friends have been honest enough to challenge Stuart on his insecure response to difficult situations.

Stuart's non-confrontational approach can be a strength at times – his willingness to be 'blurred at the edges' as Duane White puts it. It allows for a broad group of churches from different backgrounds within Ground Level. But Duane also considers there is a downside – an unwillingness to be clear when there is a need to be and an unwillingness to confront when it's needed.

Insecure with others? Occasionally. Insecure with God? No. There is a closeness in their walk with God. It is reflected in many ways – not least in a love for God's word and an awareness of the work of the Holy Spirit. Stuart pursues the Holy Spirit. He will, to this day, travel anywhere where the Holy Spirit is at work, to receive and to take what God is doing back to his local context.

John Hindmarsh, Stuart's childhood friend and fellow band member, identifies a magnetism and an openness of heart as key to Stuart and his ministry. He comments:

Stuart has never lost that ordinariness that enables him to be approachable and come alongside people. He's not ordinary of course, but he has never put himself on a pedestal. Leadership has not gone to his head. He knows his weaknesses and has built well with others to create a combinational strength that means one plus one equals ten.

Stuart's unassuming manner and ability to maintain the 'middle ground' has meant that friendships have developed with men and women in ministry well beyond the same or similar house church roots of Stuart and Irene. It is reflected in Grapevine and the One Event. Guest speakers over the years have come from many backgrounds – denominational and not. Health and prosperity teaching and its opposite. Wild prophets and cautious theologians.

Not only have these kinds of ministries worked with Stuart and Irene, but they also consider themselves friends. Jeff Lucas reflects that there was always an openness, a welcome and an empowering from Stuart that he willingly offers to other ministries. Duane White considers Stuart's confidence in the Holy Spirit as the key. Stuart listens to God and is confident in the outworking of that. Link that to the unassuming manner and there's a leadership and influence that is very effective.

Jack Groblewski calls it 'statesmanlike'. It's a big word to use, but it reflects well Stuart's ability to cross streams and denominations, to speak clearly and effectively, often with a prophetic edge, but always in a way that honours the host.

Pace and Preparation

The open door at Stuart and Irene's home has been replaced by an open door to leadership throughout the church. Discipleship of new and younger leaders is an essential part of the church and it is no surprise that this was pioneered by Stuart and Irene. Ever since the wall came down in their first home to accommodate more young people, there has been a careful discipleship model in place.

Stuart is very deliberate and methodical about this. There is both pace and preparation. His children tell the story of how he used to lead the family on their holidays. If there is a place to go, Stuart, slightly stressed, is at the front and leading at a pace. No more so than at airports when on occasion he has been walking so fast, the rest of the family have been left behind. It's happened so many times, the children have dubbed it 'Dad's airport mode'!

Preparation too. Younger son Dave advises that Stuart, when driving, will generally have the money ready for a toll booth approximately four counties earlier than actually needed.

Apply this to church, and young leaders are challenged to keep up but with every available resource ready at hand well before they are needed. The fruit is there to see. Nearly every next generation leader in and around the Lincoln church have been through this model, one that was birthed all those years ago. It is hard to overstate this. Within the DNA of Alive Church is this consistent discipleship model of younger leaders, one that Stuart and Irene learnt from the day when thirty or so young people ended up on their doorstep through the ministry of The Advocates, but with no church to go to.

Pastors' Kids

Dave tells the story of not wanting to admit at school that his father was a pastor. On more than one occasion, he announced that Dad was a bouncer. The humour is not lost on five-foot-seven-inches Stuart.

As pastors and leaders, it's hard to keep the balance between family and church activity.

Stuart feels he failed to keep that balance in the early years with The Advocates, soon after Andrew was born. Andrew did not feel the loss though – only the anticipation of Dad returning home with a present and time together. No matter how tired Stuart might be from his travels, there was always time for a game in the garden with Andrew. And with Becki too. She insisted on joining in and heading the ball back and forth with Dad.

Thursday nights were 'treat nights' for the kids growing up. Whether it was a trip out for fish and chips or playing in the park, these evenings were treasured by the children. Becki used to ask to go out to a hotel for a meal. For her, this was the pinnacle of being grown up – all part of a treat night.

Not just Thursdays either. Stuart gave up many a Saturday morning to going swimming with all three kids. Playing badminton at the local leisure centre was another favourite. Longer football sessions too, at West Common nearby.

And when church meetings went on too long, Becki remembers being allowed to stay up at the back of the hall, complete with sleeping bag.

Holidays growing up were at Bridlington – the very place Stuart used to go to as a kid. Perhaps it's a requirement of being in the Bell family? Not that the children minded. Becki has fond memories of Topham's Ice Cream Parlour – or more particularly, the contents of the parlour!

But there was one holiday destination that was definitely not on Stuart's agenda growing up – the United States. With the increased friendship with Jack and Trish Groblewski, Stuart and Irene holidayed there on a number of occasions, often mixing it with ministry, and all three children went too. It's only on reflection years later that Andrew appreciates how special that was.

Today Andrew is a successful deputy headteacher. He has been awarded the National Primary School Teacher of the Year. He's part of Alive Church and leads different activities. He attributes his calling into teaching to his experiences at Grapevine. The awareness that the Holy Spirit was leading him, together with prophetic words and encouragement from others, was a potent mix.

Becki is married to Glen and they have two children. Becki felt called to dance ministry from an early age, desperate as a young girl to be part of Ishmael's Glory Company at the Grapevine children's worship. And she has performed many times on the Grapevine stage over the years. As a child, she received a prophetic word that she would also appear on television and this has now happened a number of times. Becki has owned her own dance and drama school. She and Glen are part of the leadership team at the Lincoln North location of Alive and remain close to Mum and Dad.

Dave is on staff at Alive Church. He leads worship and has had the privilege of leading at Grapevine and the One Event on the main stage. He's a more than proficient guitar player and as a singer-songwriter, heads up the band The Moment. He retains a sense of humour that may just get him into trouble now and again. Dave is married to Sarah and they have four miracle children.

The picture here is of a family united. And a family of faith. All three children with a call to Lincoln, with a love for the fact that they are near to Mum and Dad. All three children loving hanging out with Mum and Dad as friends together – there has been a subtle shift from parenthood to friendship.

The friendship shows itself in teasing Dad for some of his idiosyncrasies. Andrew notes Stuart's propensity to always include the phrase 'at the beginning of the twenty-first century' in any talk he gives. All three children note the regularity with which he is prone to break into song. Any conversation that includes anything near a Beatles' lyric will quickly be followed by the appropriate song.

It's a hard thing to do as a Christian leader – carry your family with you. Too many pastors' kids have lost their faith along the way. By God's grace and through a lot of hard work from Stuart and Irene, that hasn't happened. And already there's a third generation of Bell's coming through into leadership.

And through it all, a happy marriage. Becki loves the fact that Mum and Dad still hold hands as they walk together. It's reflective of their love and friendship. Despite all the pressures, they have put each other first.

Stuart and Irene's legacy? Spiritual sons and daughters. Including their own three children. It includes those early pioneers. It includes the latest recruit to the Alive Church Academy programme. Young men and women starting out on an adventure with Christ could find no better mentors.

Chapter Twelve
The End Of The Beginning

Meet Bethany. She's a teenager at Alive Lincoln and is standing in the coffee queue at the final One Event. Her favourite memories of Stuart and Irene? Being there at the Easter egg hunt and giving out eggs, being great sports in the 'pegging competition' – a game where kids try and place a peg on the clothes of anyone and everyone. Being there when as a five-year-old child Bethany gave her life to Jesus Christ at Grapevine and then shared what she'd done on the main stage in the big-top. And being there when she became the youngest child to get baptised in water at Alive Church.

'I can't say I know them that well, but they are there for me and that's just really nice.'

Encouraging. Available. Challenging. The adjectives to describe them are many.

And 'nice'. Not the strongest of words for Bethany to use, but apt. They really are nice people!

The Final One Event

It nearly didn't happen. Covid. Lockdown. Would there be an appetite to meet together? Would the lockdown be ended by then?

But with boldness and a lot of prayer, a final One Event was announced.

August 28th, 2021. A one-day event at Lincolnshire Showground. And a final celebration and thanks to God for forty years of Grapevine and the One Event.

Forty years since that first step of faith in 1982. Forty years of prayer, declaration, teaching and encouragement. Leaders have stepped out into new ministries there. Churches have been born there. People have met their partners there. Possibly babies have been conceived there. We'll leave it at that.

Forty years of fashion change too. Forty years since 1982, the year of the mullet haircut. Best forgotten. But if you're of an age that has no idea what's being talked about, Google it. Yes, people really did think this was high fashion! And I was reading it's making a come-back. Surely not!

As Stuart mentioned later in the day, forty years since wearing red trousers and shaking a tambourine. According to his kids, Dad was pretty much attached to that tambourine. A crescent moon affair, to be held low in the right hand and banged against the thigh.

Are the rumours true? Did tambourines get banned from Grapevine at some time or other? They certainly interfered with the recordings of the worship. If they were banned, it was a good decision. (Stuart's children remember that along with the tambourine there was the regular two-hop dad-dance and an occasional star-jump when things got particularly exciting!)

As the crowds were welcomed onto the site and into the open arena in front of the stage, there was a degree of relief from Stuart that people had actually come to this final One Event.

It Won't Stop Now

Cars continue to arrive as worship gets under way. Banks of speakers surround the stage. Two large screens tower over the phalanx of seats spreading out on the grass and the raised mounds at the back, creating a natural amphitheatre. The volume is enough to reach the rest of the site with the various catering vans together with tents and stands for the numerous Christian charities represented today.

Matt and Claire, hosts for this first part of the day, are excitedly getting things underway. And the sun is shining – a specific answer to prayer as there is no big-top this time around.

Looking over the gathering, grey hair predominates. There are youngsters though – loads of them – with their own activities as well.

Solid drums and strong rhythms introduce everyone to the reason they are there.

'Now I'm ready, Lord, ready for whatever you want to do,' declares Matt.

Appropriate words at the start of the day when one era ends and another begins.

The last. Forty years of Grapevine and the One Event. A day of honouring, declaring, seeking, hearing His voice.

Dave Bell, guitar in hand, invites everyone to stand.

Hands are raised. There's dancing, shouting, singing, declarations of who God is and what He has done. Declarations of a breakthrough coming. Something that won't stop.

And that's the truth. It won't stop. In the end Covid could not stop this event. Just a day. But what a day. As the virus wanes, the gathered congregation sing and shout it out.

It won't stop now.

The One Event may stop now, but surely there is more. Much more.

As the worship continues, Stuart is leaning forward, on tiptoe, arms raised as high as he can, declaring the words of the song.

It won't stop now.

Old and New

The day is a beautiful mix of the old and new. An honouring of those who pioneered and a declaration over the new generation for more to come.

Dave Bell gives way to Chris Bowater as he leads in songs from yesteryear, but still prophetic for tomorrow.

'This song is called "Faithful God",' says Chris, 'for those in the silent world, in the death and the darkness they are trapped in. There is One who is faithful.'

The old and new theme continues throughout the day. Ishmael is there with a full-on Glories party, as much for the grown-ups as for the kids. There's a medley of Christian artists through the worship times including Graham Kendrick, Lurine Cato, Lou Fellingham, Philippa Hanna, Tom Smith, Jake Isaac and Noel Robinson.

Paul Benger, pointing to the future, takes the first talk. Always honouring history but very clearly pointing the way forward.

Jeff Lucas is there: 'Grapevine and the One Event have helped us identify – with each other and with our God who is greater than the pressures around us.'

The final talk comes, appropriately, from Stuart.

We have one day to remember forty years. The Greek word *Chronos* is the gift of time; the Greek word *Kairos* is a God-given time. We have enjoyed a *Kairos*, a God-given time.

From that first Grapevine with borrowed equipment and a thousand people – no bookings in those days. We weren't sure anyone would come.

The church landscape has changed over these forty years. We have seen the phenomenal growth of contemporary worship. We have seen a people of the Word becoming also a people of the Spirit.

Forty years is mentioned 146 times in the Bible. Often it relates to the end of a test or trial. Israel were forty years in the wilderness. David and Solomon each reigned over Israel for forty years until their generation ended. In a sense, our forty-year generation is ending.

Each summer has been taken up with this showground. The constant conversation has been whether it will rain or not. It's time to pass on the baton. Not to get nostalgic but to be prophetic . . .

Stuart goes on to reflect on the early years. There are name checks for Jean Darnall and Gerald Coates. There's thanks for every person in every team who has served over the years.

Cross in the Sky

And as Stuart speaks, a beautiful thing happens in the skies. The sun has been setting to the west, and as it does so the rays pick up a couple of vapour trails from passing aircraft. The effect is to paint a cross in the sky.

'We have enjoyed high levels of unity and friendship,' says Stuart. 'There has been some "friendly fire", or not so friendly fire if I'm honest, but my reflection on these forty years is one of friends together. Thank you, my friends.'

Earlier there had been a fly-past from the Red Arrows, housed at a nearby airfield. And the final farewell was to be a firework display. But before that – before Stuart spoke in fact – there was what, in retrospect, was to be a key moment of the day: an honouring of Stuart and Irene. As prayers were prayed and prophetic words spoken, Pete Atkins, friend and leader with Stuart and Irene for many years, came onto the stage to read over them a moving and reflective declaration:

As the current Ground Level team, we feel it right to take a moment within this fortieth celebration, to honour the part Stuart and Irene have played in this, over four decades of time. This gathering today, however strange the circumstances, is about celebrating what God has done over forty years and looking ahead to the future in Him. It's a day to praise, worship and thank God for His goodness and faithfulness over the years and to set our hearts and faces to a new future as He calls us on. This future is one where He becomes known to so many more, where He brings His transformation to the world we live in and brings about His kingdom.

On this day, it is right and proper to honour Stuart and Irene for their huge part in founding and leading this event over forty years. This event has been a space in which hundreds – thousands – of people have come to know Jesus, where hundreds – thousands – have been filled with His Spirit, where there has been a life-giving flow of healing, restoration to God and each other, inspiration and equipping. In this space, hundreds of children and young people have had the course of their lives changed as they have discovered Jesus and started a lifetime of following Him. At this event, many, many, have heard God calling them to ministry; many have chosen their course in life in an immense variety of spheres. In the economy of God this event has played its part in the shaping of the Church.

And today we thank God for the part Stuart and Irene have played: their faith, their perseverance, their inspiration, their preparedness to count the cost, their steadfastness in the face of opposition, their pursuit of the radical middle ground, of unity, of partnership, of relationship, of Word and Spirit. We have seen their response in praise and worship to the moving of God in this place.

We have also seen their faithfulness and vulnerability when the challenges have come. We have seen them stand even when the 'wobbly bit in the middle' [an Irene phrase] has been around them. In this rather public space, they have faced the destructive threat of hurricanes – the winds so strong that tents have disappeared – they have trusted God in persistent horrible weather and the stands collapsing. They have stood in God in the face of betrayal by friends, in the very public midst of life-threatening illness of one of their children and indeed the passing away of Graham, Stuart's brother, at the time of the One Event. They have stood under criticism for being too accommodating of views either end of the theological spectrum and of making space for people who would not usually share a platform. They have been criticised for the risks taken with particular speakers or worship styles or pricing structures or organisational glitches. They have stood in faith under the pressure every year of the need to make the finances of the event work – with costs covered and still able to bless ministries we are in relationship with. Nevertheless, in both the wonderful times, the amazing times of the presence and moving of God and in the painful difficult times they have remained firm in God.

So today we honour them, not for being perfect but for their leadership and faithfulness exercised in humility under the mighty hand of God. We thank God for them, not in some kind of idolatry, but in heartfelt gratitude for their example of allowing God to work through their humanity and bless countless others.

Stuart and Irene, thank you for what you have made possible in God. Thank you for the cost you have faced. Thank you for the example of leadership.

Thank you for holding the radical middle ground, for demonstrating Spirit and Word, for demonstrating the priority of relationship and partnership without ownership, for practical unity, for never taking our focus away from looking to God and for the moving of God in revival in our land.

Thank you for your love for the whole Church and for the local church – teaching its importance in God's mission and presence in the world.

Thank you for being faithful to those in other parts of the world God has connected us with, and to partners and friends in this country.

Thank you for faithful service over the forty years that lie behind us, and which now become an amazing platform from which to reach for our future in God.

Applause

As Pete Atkins finishes reading the written declaration, there is spontaneous applause. Others join him to pray for Stuart and Irene. As everyone stands, hands raised in blessing towards them, there is a moment of silence. A reflective moment. A 'this is where we have been' moment. An awareness of God's goodness and thanks for the faithful couple who listened and obeyed.

Stuart's comments in his final talk were similar. Who knew what was about to happen that time Jean Darnall came to tea? The prophetic words she spoke, the call on Stuart's life to be an apostle of churches, of a whole movement, have been worked out in the purposes of God for forty years and more.

The 'more' is important. As Stuart ends his talk, there is a call to the more. To the next generation. A *Kairos* moment. A God-given time. A time to have shared the stories as in Jewish culture. A time to remember what God has done. And a time to push forward. Stuart continues:

> The law says 'choose life' (Deuteronomy 30:19). The prophets say 'follow Him' (1 Kings 18:21). The gospel says 'repent' (Acts 2:38). We have been given a day. A day to celebrate forty years. But God is moving on. There's more life to choose, more following Him and more repentance to declare. There's a shift taking place. Keep moving forward. Remain pioneers. It's time to push forward into all God has for us. There are many adventures ahead. We serve a God who has intervened in history and who will continue to do so. Say to God 'I'm available' and see what He will do!

As Stuart steps away from the microphone, people stand to their feet. The applause goes on. And on.

The end of the beginning.

END-PIECE BY STUART BELL

On the day we celebrated our Golden Wedding anniversary, Irene and I were taking a break in our favourite hotel in Harrogate when we heard the news of Gerald Coates' passing. Were it not for Gerald's prophetic 'nudge' this book would never have been written. In fact, when Gerald phoned during the Covid lockdown, pretty much the last thing on my agenda was the telling of our story. However, through the years I have learnt to trust his insights. Over the same weekend Christine Noble, known for her creative prophetic ministry, also went to be with the Lord, and Arthur Mann (mentioned in this book) died at the age of ninety three.

As I write this end-piece I am aware of the changing landscape of the church across the world and how fleeting life can seem. We do need to keep telling the stories of God's faithfulness from one generation to the next. I want to use these final words to express my thanks to many who have shared the journey. My life and ministry have been tied with so many faithful friends and colleagues.

I begin with thanks to my family. Irene has been faithfully alongside through all my ministry. She has been my best supporter, loyal friend and most honest critic. I could not have made the journey without her love and commitment. I'm grateful

God gifted us with wonderful children: Andrew, Rebekah and David, plus Glen and Sarah – near-perfect in-laws. Grandparents to Jermac, Trenton, Jackson, Levi, Mayah and Sophia, we couldn't be more fulfilled, especially as they all live close by and are part of our church family.

Thanks are also due to Ann (Irene's sister) and Dave, and to Elizabeth (Stuart's sister) and Dave. I'm very proud of Elizabeth 'Diz' and Dave, who have pioneered an excellent church, The Storehouse, in Skegness, an amazing resource for the east coast.

I'm grateful for many individuals, both in our local church setting and our Ground Level network. Through the years many have been involved so I limit the list to those alongside now, though many more remain in my memory with gratitude.

Thanks go to Howard and Claire Williams, Paul and Joy Blundell, Dan and Jo Hargreaves, Jonas and Sian Eyles, together with Location and Life Pastors within Alive Church.

Many have served Ground Level but I particularly mention Paul and Jeannie Benger who are now leading the team.

Nationally I am grateful to Partners For Influence, a group of leaders who have met together twice a year for friendship, input and encouragement. Steve and Angie Campbell have led alongside us for a number of years.

Irene and I have also been honoured to be part of the Richmond group led by Nicky and Pippa Gumbel. Wider fruitful relationships include Jack and Trish Groblewski, Dan and Ronda Backens, Louis and Natasja Kotzé, Dave and Karen Smith, Duane and Kris White.

Our thanks go to the Milligan family and Rise Church for their kindness shown towards David during his last operation.

Finally, thank you Ralph for listening to my many words, for your willingness to take on this project, and for the sensitive way both you and Roh let us share our pains and joys, tears and laughter.

As we have emerged out of two years of Covid, and as people have ventured back into Church life, I must confess that the early morning runs have slowed down somewhat, but hopefully passion for the Church of Jesus is as strong as ever.

It is a joy to see people we have invested our lives in succeeding in ministry and we look forward in anticipation to the days ahead, knowing that what God began, He will complete. We are still expecting a great move of the Holy Spirit in our lifetime and we join with Jesus' words: 'Your kingdom come, Your will be done on earth, as it is in heaven.'

On 23rd July 2022, the Emmanuel Centre in Marsham Street, London, was filled with people celebrating the life and ministry of Gerald Coates. A number of tributes were brought. I had the honour, along with others, of bringing such a tribute. It was a strange feeling, meeting people who I had not seen for over thirty years. Irene and I met Jeff and Kay Lucas prior to this gathering and we found ourselves talking about our past memories. We reflected on how quickly time has moved on and shared a little about our apprehensions for facing the challenges of old age. It was noticeable that very few young leaders were present at the gathering. As the gathering finished, Anona Coates was honoured and flowers were presented. People then gathered together in the adjacent hall where wine was available and conversations were shared.

This reminded me that at the close of most special friendship gatherings, Gerald would raise his glass and wait for a few seconds before we raised ours. Then, with a broad smile on his face, he would say, 'To the King and the Kingdom.'

As Irene and I were on the train returning home we felt a renewed need not only to honour history but also to continue to build for the generations ahead.

And so, to you the reader, God's blessing upon you and may all we do always be . . . to the King and the Kingdom.

Stuart.

BOOKS BY STUART BELL

In Search of Revival – A Guide for Everyone Who Wants More

Rebuilding the Walls – A Challenge to the Church from Ezra and Nehemiah

Mud in the Eye (with Dave Bell)

Accolade – A Special Acknowledgement of the Life and Ministry of John Phillips

The Name – A Journey Through the Names and Character of God

BOOKS BY RALPH TURNER

Working for God

God-Life

Cheating Death, Living Life – Linda's Story (with Linda Huskisson)

Gerald Coates – Pioneer

The Power Partnership (with Jonathan Conrathe)

Faith Man – Wild Adventures with a Faithful God (with David Lamb)

Greater Things – The Story of New Wine (with Paul Harcourt)

Embrace the Journey – Becky Murray's Story (with Becky Murray)

Returning the Lost Smiles – One Man's Fight Against Leprosy (with Amar Timalsina)

Compelling – The Fight for a Faith School (with Dr Cheron Byfield)

ABOUT THE AUTHOR

Ralph Turner is a Christian author specialising in biographies and ghost-written autobiographies. Ralph and Rohini are based in Leicester. They are part of the team at Chroma Church Leicester and Ralph also serves as Team Pastor for Mission24. You can find out more at **www.mountain50.blogspot.com**

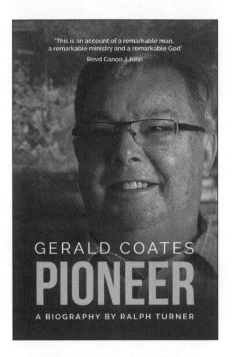

GERALD COATES

PIONEER

A BIOGRAPHY BY RALPH TURNER

Gerald Coates was different. A pastor, a pioneer and a provocateur. His bold prophetic ministry, both in terms of speaking prophetically and in terms of living that way, challenged the established church.

This book celebrates Gerald's life and brings a message that is just as relevant to the church today. You may not know it, but if you live in the UK, your church and your locality have more than likely been affected in some way by Gerald's ministry!

This book will inspire and encourage you. Along the way, you will meet some amazing people. Some famous. Some less well known. But all important to a story that has helped change the church as we know it.

To order a copy scan the code below

Compelling
The Fight for a Faith School

Dr Cheron Byfield and Ralph Turner

A compelling vision. An impossible challenge. A gracious God. A journey from vision to reality starts with a step. A step into controversy, politics, backstabbing and lies. A step into achievement, success, thanksgiving and worship. This is the story of the fight for a Faith School. This is the King Solomon story.

To order a copy scan the code below